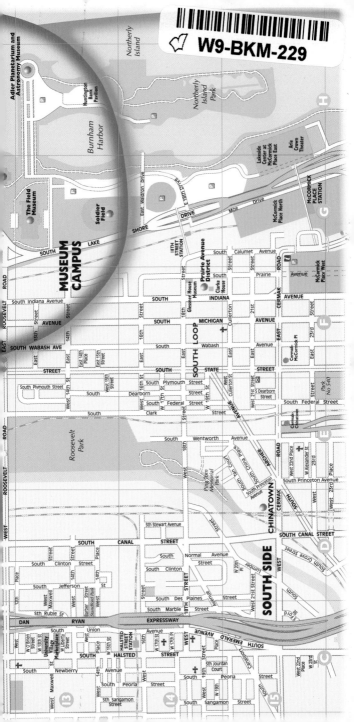

W9-BKM-229

Fodor's
25 Best

CHICAGO

How to Use This Book

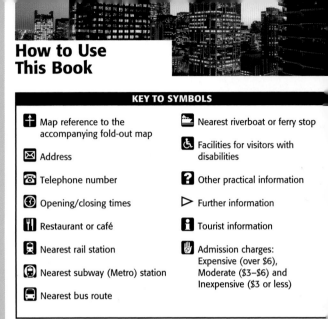

KEY TO SYMBOLS

✚	Map reference to the accompanying fold-out map	⛴	Nearest riverboat or ferry stop
✉	Address	♿	Facilities for visitors with disabilities
☎	Telephone number	❓	Other practical information
🕓	Opening/closing times	▷	Further information
🍴	Restaurant or café	🛈	Tourist information
🚆	Nearest rail station	✋	Admission charges: Expensive (over $6), Moderate ($3–$6) and Inexpensive ($3 or less)
Ⓜ	Nearest subway (Metro) station		
🚌	Nearest bus route		

This guide is divided into four sections

● Essential Chicago: An introduction to the city and tips on making the most of your stay.

● Chicago by Area: We've broken the city into five areas, and recommended the best sights, shops, entertainment venues, nightlife and places to eat in each one. Suggested walks help you to explore on foot.

● Where to Stay: The best hotels, whether you're looking for luxury, budget or something in between.

● Need to Know: The info you need to make your trip run smoothly, including getting about by public transportation, weather tips, emergency phone numbers and useful websites.

Navigation In the Chicago by Area chapter, we've given each area its own color, which is also used on the locator maps throughout the book and the map on the inside front cover.

Maps The fold-out map accompanying this book is a comprehensive street plan of Chicago. The grid on this fold-out map is the same as the grid on the locator maps within the book. We've given grid references within the book for each sight and listing.

Contents

ESSENTIAL CHICAGO	4–18
Introducing Chicago	4–5
A Short Stay in Chicago	6–7
Top 25	8–9
Shopping	10–11
Shopping by Theme	12
Chicago by Night	13
Where to Eat	14
Where to Eat by Cuisine	15
Top Tips For...	16–18

CHICAGO BY AREA	19–106
THE LOOP	20–38
Area map	22–23
Sights	24–31
Walk	32
Shopping	33–34
Entertainment and Nightlife	35–36
Where to Eat	37–38

MUSEUM CAMPUS	39–54
Area map	40–41
Sights	42–51
Walk	52
Entertainment and Nightlife	53
Where to Eat	54

NORTH SIDE	55–80
Area map	56–57
Sights	58–72
Walk	73
Shopping	74–75
Entertainment and Nightlife	76–78
Where to Eat	78–80

SOUTH SIDE	81–94
Area map	82–83
Sights	84–91
Walk	92
Entertainment and Nightlife	93
Where to Eat	94

FARTHER AFIELD	95–106
Area map	96–97
Sights	98–102
Shopping	103
Entertainment and Nightlife	104
Where to Eat	106

WHERE TO STAY	107–112
Introduction	108
Budget Hotels	109
Mid-Range Hotels	110–111
Luxury Hotels	112

NEED TO KNOW	113–125
Planning Ahead	114–115
Getting There	116–117
Getting Around	118–119
Essential Facts	120–123
Timeline	124–125

CONTENTS

Introducing Chicago

Poet Carl Sandburg called Chicago "City of the big shoulders." Former Mayor Richard J. Daley boasted it's "the city that works." It's nicknamed "The Windy City," not because of its weather, but because of its long-winded politicians. Pick your interpretation— city of brawn and industry, brash and bustling, modern and innovative—it's all here in Chicago.

In the 1800s, as the city grew, a distinct breed of entrepreneurs and hucksters made their way to the city's Lake Michigan shores seeking opportunity. No amount of tragedy could persuade them from their enterprises, be they legal or not. Two days after the Great Chicago Fire of 1871 had reduced most of the city to ashes, one real-estate broker posted a sign reading: "All gone but wife, children and energy."

Afterward, the city shucked its 19th-century past and became the most modern metropolis in the country, if not the world, home to the first skyscraper and a new Prairie School of architecture in sync with the low, limitless horizon of the region. Musicians came and amped up the blues. Gangsters grabbed a piece of the action and held on. Immigrants flocked here from every corner of the world, bringing their culture and foods to Chicago's neighborhoods. Everyone thought big. "Make no little plans," said former Chicago city planner and architect Daniel Burnham, "they have no magic to stir men's blood."

The spirit of optimism that marks the commercial aspects of the city is distinct on a personal level, too. It's a common stereotype that Midwesterners are friendly; Chicagoans are often that and much more—honest, opinionated and nice. It takes optimism to emigrate and Chicago received wave after wave of Scandinavians and Germans early on, later welcoming large communities of Irish, Polish and Mexicans. Chicago is perhaps the most American city of all.

FACTS AND FIGURES

- Residents: 2.72 million
- Languages spoken: 150
- Museums: 80
- Parks: 601
- Third largest city in the US
- Lakefront bike paths: 18 miles (29km)
- The "Historic Route 66" begins in downtown Chicago on Adams Street, in front of the Art Institute of Chicago.

MUSICAL CHICAGO

Jazz has thrived in the city since the 1920s when New Orleans' innovators moved north. Louis Armstrong struck out on his own with the "Hot Five" recordings he made in town. Later, African-Americans moving up from the rural South settled in and took the traditional blues music electric. Both jazz and blues clubs still entertain today.

EDIBLE CHICAGO

In the early 20th century, Chicago was a meat-and-potatoes town, home of stockyards and slaughterhouses and the railroad hub transporting beef to the outer regions. Steak houses, deep-dish pizza and hot dogs continue the tradition of substantive eating in Chicago. But in the past 25 years the city has nurtured a modern band of chefs to become one of the most innovative places to eat in the US.

DESIGN CHICAGO

Architects and entrepreneurs engineered Chicago's phoenix after the Great Fire, inventing the skyscraper in the rebuilding. Daniel Burnham had bold plans for Chicago's front yard of parks that buffer city and shore. Frank Lloyd Wright founded his Prairie School of design here. Later innovators such as Mies van der Rohe also left their mark and bolstered Chicago's reputation as a great architectural town.

A Short Stay in Chicago

DAY 1

Morning Start your stay with a 9am stroll around **Millennium Park** (▷ 50), then walk across Frank Gehry's bridge to see and photograph the reflections on the highly polished bean-shape sculpture by Anish Kapoor.

Mid-morning Walk the two blocks over to the **Art Institute of Chicago** (▷ 44). Doors open at 10.30 most days, 10 on weekends, and lines form at least 15 minutes prior. It's worth the effort to have the Impressionist galleries briefly to yourself.

Lunch Take a break and soak up the Loop atmosphere at **Atwood** (▷ 37), just a few blocks northwest of the museum on Washington and State streets.

Afternoon Head to Randolph and Wabash, where you can catch the elevated train, aka the **El** (▷ 26). Take the Brown Line bound for Kimball. Get off at the Belmont stop and walk to the opposite platform to catch the train heading back to the Loop.

Mid-afternoon Take a leisurely walk around the **Loop** to admire some public sculpture installed there (▷ 25). Start your walk with the unnamed Picasso in Daley Center Plaza, then continue on to the Calder at the Federal Center Plaza and, finally, see the Jean Dubuffet at the James R. Thompson Center.

Dinner Head for **Gino's East** (▷ panel, 80) for an authentic taste of Chicago's deep-dish pizza.

Evening Get tickets to **Second City** (▷ 67) for a good guffaw over Chicago-style humor, which is topical and partly improvised.

DAY 2

Morning Hop on the 10am **Architecture Foundation River Cruise**
(▷ 24) offered by the Chicago Architecture Foundation. The tours are a
big draw and usually sell out so reserve before coming to town.

Mid-morning Disembark the boat and walk up the **Magnificent Mile**
(▷ 68), the stretch of Michigan Avenue that runs from the Chicago River
up to Oak Street, to check out the upscale shopping district with its
exclusive boutiques, street performers, and a number of architectural
landmarks including the **Wrigley Building** (▷ 72), **Tribune Tower**
(▷ 72) and the **John Hancock Center** (▷ 58–59).

Lunch Stop for an upscale burger and a locally brewed beer at **South
Water Kitchen** (▷ 38), a good spot for Midwestern comfort food.

Afternoon Rent bikes at **Navy Pier** (▷ 64) and take a spin on the Lake
Michigan shoreline past the popular **Oak Street** (▷ 71) and **North
Avenue** (▷ 66) beaches to appreciate how Chicagoans play.

Mid-afternoon Ascend the John Hancock building to **360 Chicago**
(▷ 58) to see the city from 1,000ft (305m) above the ground. If you
dare, try TILT, the new thrill experience where you stand in a glass box
and tilt over the edge of the skyscraper.

Dinner Sit down to order a sampling of wine perfectly paired to entrées
as well as small, shareable plates at the innovative wine bar and café
Bin 36 (▷ 78).

Evening Take a cab to **Buddy Guy's Legends** (▷ 86) on the near South
Side to catch a few sets of the blues before calling it a night.

▼▼▼ **360 Chicago** ▷ **58–59** See for miles around from this perfect viewpoint.

Adler Planetarium and Astronomy Museum ▷ **42–43** The nation's first planetarium.

Art Institute of Chicago ▷ **44–45** Leading fine art museum with a collection of art and photography.

Biking on the Chicago Lakefront ▷ **84** Paved paths reserved for bikes, skates and strollers.

Boutique Browsing in Wicker Park/Bucktown ▷ **99** Small, independent, cutting-edge shops.

Chicago Architecture Foundation River Cruise ▷ **24** Docents lead tours of Chicago's famed skyline.

DuSable Museum of African American History ▷ **85** A leader among this type of institution.

The Field Museum ▷ **46–47** Sprawling museum exhibits the world's largest T. rex.

Frank Lloyd Wright Home and Studio ▷ **100** A concentration of Lloyd Wright buildings.

Gallery Hopping in River North ▷ **60–61** Art galleries in former industrial redbrick warehouses.

Hitting a Blues Club ▷ **86** The beat goes on in live music clubs.

John G. Shedd Aquarium ▷ **48–49** Houses nearly 8,000 denizens of the deep.

Lincoln Park Zoo ▷ **62–63** Popular zoo in the heart of the park and residential district.

Loop Public Sculpture ▷ **25** Chicago is renowned for its public sculpture.

Millennium Park ▷ **50** Garden sculpture and monumental stage architecture by Frank Gehry.

Museum of Science and Industry ▷ **88–89** Claims 35,000 artifacts, many of which are interactive.

Navy Pier ▷ **64–65** Chicago's most popular attraction is part-carnival and part-cultural enclave.

North Avenue Beach ▷ **66** Best-equipped beach of the 31 that line the lakefront. ▼▼▼

Prairie Avenue District ▷ **87** Grand Victorian homes line the avenue.

Riding the El Train ▷ **26** Two stories above street level, the El offers rapid transit with views.

The Rookery ▷ **27** This 1888 landmark features a skylit lobby renovated by Frank Lloyd Wright.

Second City ▷ **67** Chicago's original improvisational comedy theater still hosts hilarious shows.

Shopping the Magnificent Mile ▷ **68** Michigan Avenue's toniest stretch, with leading stores.

Willis Tower ▷ **28–29** Chicago's third-tallest building offers observation deck views to surrounding states.

Wrigley Field ▷ **101** Spend a day enjoying the US's favorite game.

These pages are a quick guide to the Top 25, which are described in more detail later. Here they are listed alphabetically and the tinted background shows the area they are in.

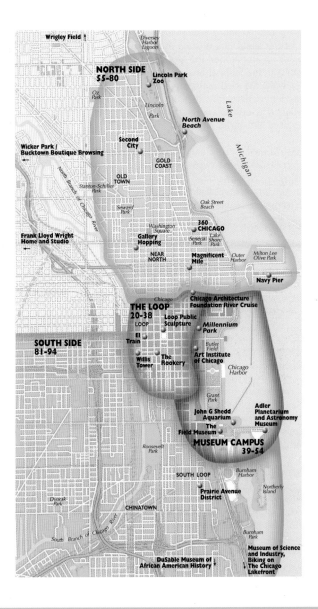

Wrigley Field ↑

Diversey Harbor Lagoon

NORTH SIDE 55–80

Lincoln Park Zoo

Oz Park

Lincoln Park

North Avenue Beach

Lake Michigan

Wicker Park / Bucktown Boutique Browsing

Second City

Stanton-Schiller Park

GOLD COAST

OLD TOWN

North Branch of Chicago River

Seward Park

Oak Street Beach

Frank Lloyd Wright Home and Studio

Washington Square

Gallery Hopping

360 CHICAGO

Seneca Park

Lake Shore Park

Milton Lee Olive Park

NEAR NORTH

Magnificent Mile

Outer Harbor

Navy Pier

Chicago

Chicago Architecture Foundation River Cruise

THE LOOP 20–38

LOOP

Loop Public Sculpture

Millennium Park

El Train

Butler Field

Art Institute of Chicago

SOUTH SIDE 81–94

Willis Tower

The Rookery

Chicago Harbor

Grant Park

John G Shedd Aquarium

Adler Planetarium and Astronomy Museum

The Field Museum

MUSEUM CAMPUS 39–54

Roosevelt Park

Burnham Harbor

Northerly Island

SOUTH LOOP

Prairie Avenue District

Dvorak Park

CHINATOWN

Burnham Park

South Branch of Chicago River

Museum of Science and Industry, Biking on The Chicago Lakefront

DuSable Museum of African American History

ESSENTIAL CHICAGO TOP 25

9

Shopping

Chicago's shops can excite the purchasing passions of the entire Midwest while surprising and delighting visitors from much farther afield. The upscale malls and boutiques on and around the Magnificent Mile attest to the international nature of the city, while the plethora of smaller independent outlets show that the city has retained its own character against the onslaught of globalized retailing.

Shopping Streets

For designer clothing, the Magnificent Mile is the showplace of Chicago. Men and women in pursuit of quality attire will find most major names represented in the high-rise malls along Michigan Avenue. For those who prefer a more personal shopping experience, a stroll around nearby Oak Street finds a clutch of elegant boutiques offering European haute couture and eager sales assistants. The same area hosts many of the city's major art galleries and antiques dealers. Venture out into the city's neighborhoods, and you'll find small, chic, funky or eco-friendly boutiques.

Antiques and Retro

More fine art and antiques dealers can be found in River North, while their brasher, funkier counterparts are a feature in the shopping districts of Lake View and Wicker Park. There is also an abundance of outlets for clothing, both new and vintage, and places to purchase a range of household furnishings, including some bizarre items, often made by local craftspeople.

ENTERTAINMENT IN MALLS

Many downtown Chicago malls are more than just places to shop. They also have entertainment. The Water Tower Place mall has a Chicago Sports Museum on its top floor, and the Block 37 mall, on State Street, houses an AMC movie theater. The Shops at 900 N. Michigan Avenue have three high-end spas within the mall.

Chicago's extensive range of shopping options, from designer names to smaller independent stores

Souvenirs

Simple souvenirs can be found at the Magnificent Mile stores, but more choices at better prices can be found among the touristy shops of Navy Pier. Besides miniatures of high-rise buildings, such as Willis Tower, you can snatch up T-shirts, plates and fridge magnets bearing images of the skyline seen from Lake Michigan. Quirkier items, like a "Bean" bottle opener or an Al Capone bobblehead, can be found at the Accent Chicago store (▷ 75) on the top floor of Water Tower Place.

Tasty Reminders

Sausages might seem an unlikely reminder of Chicago but the city has been shaped by people of Eastern European descent, so hand-made sausages made with various meats, flavorings and spices, are a feature of many delis and restaurants. Chicago's famous deep-dish pizza also can be bought and shipped (within the US) from restaurants like Lou Malnati's and Gino's East.

Books and Music

Surviving the rising tide of international chains, Chicago retains an impressive number of independent bookstores; 57th Street in Hyde Park holds several. Likewise, the city's strong jazz and blues pedigree is represented by specialist CD and vinyl outlets often featuring new Chicago-based musicians alongside established names.

SPORTING SOUVENIRS

Chicago is a serious sports town, with several championship teams and legendary players, including basketball star Michael Jordan. The biggest hub of sports souvenir stores is around Wrigley Field. While you'll find mostly Chicago Cubs merchandise there, they also sell T-shirts and jerseys of other local and national teams. The city's most popular teams are the Cubs and White Sox (baseball), the Blackhawks (hockey), the Bulls (basketball) and the Bears (American football).

Shopping by Theme

Whether you're looking for a department store, a quirky boutique or something in between, you'll find it all in Chicago. On this page shops are listed by theme. For a more detailed write-up, see the individual listings in Chicago by Area.

Accessories
The Alley (▷ 103)
Beatnix (▷ 103)
Belmont Army Surplus (▷ 103)
Bourdage Pearls (▷ 74)
Stitch (▷ 99)

Art and Antiques
Arts & Artisans (▷ 33)
Atlas Galleries (▷ 74)
Broadway Antiques Market (▷ 103)
Illinois Artisans Shop (▷ 34)
Pagoda Red (▷ 99)
P.O.S.H. (▷ 75)
Poster Plus (▷ 34)
Randolph Street Market (▷ panel, 74)

Books
Booksamillion (▷ 33)
The Book Table (▷ 103)
Chicago Architecture Foundation (▷ 33)
Graham Crackers Comics (▷ 34)
Unabridged Bookstore (▷ 103)

Clothes and Shoes
Banana Republic (▷ 74)
Brooks Brothers (▷ 74)
City Soles (▷ 99)
Current/Elliott (▷ 99)
J. Crew (▷ 75)
Le Thrift Consignment Boutique (▷ 103)
P45 (▷ 99)
Ragstock (▷ 99)
Saint Alfred (▷ 103)
Syd Jerome (▷ 34)

Discount Outlets
DSW Shoe Warehouse (▷ 103)

Home
Elements (▷ 74)

Malls and Department Stores
900 North Michigan (▷ 74)
The Atrium Mall (▷ 33)
The Jeweler's Center (▷ 34)
Macy's (▷ 34)
Navy Pier (▷ 75)
Neiman-Marcus (▷ 75)

Saks Fifth Avenue (▷ 75)
Shops at the Mart (▷ 75)
Water Tower Place (▷ 75)

Miscellaneous
American Girl Place (▷ 74)
Art Institute of Chicago Museum Shop (▷ 33)
Blick Art Materials (▷ 33)
Dylan's Candy Bar (▷ 33)
Kokorokoko (▷ 74)
Sephora Michigan Avenue (▷ 34)

Chicago by Night

After sunset, much of the Magnificent Mile (▷ 68) and parts of the Loop are bathed in twinkling lights. The Wrigley Building (▷ 72), seen from Michigan Avenue Bridge, is famously stunning, while the illuminated profile of the John Hancock Center makes the building seem even taller. From 360 Chicago (▷ 58–59), or the Willis Tower (▷ 28–29), a nighttime viewing reveals the grid-style patterns of city neighborhoods stretching into the distance and the deep blackness of Lake Michigan dotted by the lights of ships.

Warm Nights

Warm nights during spring, summer and fall find Chicagoans outdoors, making the most of bars and restaurants with patio tables. With its hotels and late-opening shops, the Magnificent Mile is lively after dark, but there is more taking place in the nightlife strips of residential neighborhoods. The Gold Coast sections of Division, Oak and Elm streets are worth a look, as are the main drags of Wicker Park and Lake View. More commercially oriented nightlife is found amid the theme bars and clubs of River North. The cool breezes and live music at Navy Pier make a summertime stroll a must.

Winter Wonders

Cold and snowy Chicago may sometimes be, but dull it never is. The winter period marks a high point of the cultural calendar with the classical concert, opera and ballet seasons fully into their stride, as well as a complete program of theater, rock and pop music.

There are plenty of clubs and theaters to keep visitors entertained after dark

CHICAGO BLUES

The former Chess Records recording studio, where some of the biggest names in blues recorded their songs, was recently converted into Willie Dixon's Blues Heaven Foundation, a small blues museum that pays homage to the genre's history and music. It occasionally hosts small, free, top-notch concerts.

Where to Eat

Chicago is a city of hearty appetites, so guaranteeing you a good meal whether at a local hot-dog stand or at a marquee restaurant. Headquarters to the nation's slaughter-houses in the 19th century, Chicago is famed for its steak houses, such as the classic Gene & Georgetti's, and beef sandwich stands. It's now emerged as a leader in fine dining, with celebrated meals from top chefs Rick Bayless (Frontera Grill and Topolobampo), Stephanize Izard (Girl and the Goat, Little Goat Diner), and next-generation culinary experimenter Grant Achatz (Alinea and Next).

Ethnic Eats

Immigrant neighborhoods of Poles, Indians, Vietnamese, Chinese and Italians, among others, lay their tables richly with authentic homeland foods; visit Milwaukee Avenue for Polish borscht, Devon Street for Indian dal, Argyle Street for Vietnamese pho, Greektown's Halsted Street for saganaki or Chinatown for dim sum. Tasty and often thrifty adventures with myriad dining choices line those streets.

Deep-Dish Pizza

Chicago's famous deep-dish pizza consists of a pie-shaped pizza crust filled with mozzarella cheese, your choice of meat and vegetables, and topped with a heaping amount of Italian-flavored tomato sauce. Unlike New York-styled pizza, which is thin and flat, a single slice of deep-dish pizza can be a meal in itself.

CHICAGO-STYLE HOT DOGS

Chicago-style hot dogs are sold in hundreds of restaurants across the city. To eat one like a true Chicagoan, you must never put ketchup on it. Instead, find a restaurant that sells Vienna Beef brand hot dogs and order it with mustard, bright green relish, chopped onions, tomatoes, a pickle and sport peppers. Plus celery salt. Eat it on a steamed poppy-seed bun and with a side of french fries—where ketchup "is" allowed.

Dine at one of the city's superb restaurants or try Chicago's famed deep-dish pizza

Where to Eat by Cuisine

There are plenty of places to eat to suit all tastes and budgets in Chicago. On this page they are listed by cuisine. For a more detailed description of each restaurant, see Chicago by Area.

Asian
Arun's (▷ 106)
Big Bowl Café (▷ 78)
Emperor's Choice (▷ 94)
Phoenix (▷ 94)

Contemporary American
Alinea (▷ 78)
Atwood (▷ 37)
Bin 36 (▷ 78)
Columbus Tap (▷ 54)
Doves Luncheonette (▷ 79)
Exchequer (▷ 37)
McKinlock Court Restaurant (▷ 54)
Park Grill (▷ 54)
South Water Kitchen (▷ 38)
Tavern at the Park (▷ 54)

East European
Barbakan Restaurant (▷ 106)
Russian Tea Time (▷ 38)

Eclectic
Flo & Santos (▷ 94)
Grand Lux Café (▷ 79)
Pub Royale (▷ 80)
Seven on State (▷ 38)

French
Bistro Campagne (▷ 106)
Bistronomic (▷ 79)
Everest (▷ 37)
La Petite Folie (▷ 94)

German
The Berghoff (▷ 37)
Chicago Brauhaus (▷ 106)

Italian
312 Chicago (▷ 37)
Club Lucky (▷ 106)
Gino's East (▷ panel, 80)
Gioco (▷ 94)
Giordano's (▷ panel, 80)
Il Porcellino (▷ 79)
The Italian Village Restaurants (▷ 37)
Maggiano's Little Italy (▷ 80)
Petterino's (▷ 38)
Pizzeria Uno (▷ panel, 80)
Rosebud on Rush (▷ 80)
RPM Italian (▷ 38)
Trattoria No. 10 (▷ 38)

Mexican
Adobo Grill (▷ 78)
Frontera Grill/Topolobampo (▷ 79)
Xoco (▷ 80)

Middle Eastern
Noon-o-Kabab (▷ 106)
Sultan's Market (▷ 80)

Quick Bites
Chicago's Home of Chicken and Waffles (▷ 94)
Lou Mitchell's (▷ 38)
Manny's Deli & Cafeteria (▷ 94)
Portillo's Hot Dogs & Barnelli's Salad Bowl (▷ 38)
Soundings Café (▷ 54)

Seafood
Riva (▷ 80)

Steak, Ribs and Chops
Bavette's bar & Boeuf (▷ 37)
Gene & Georgetti (▷ 79)
Morton's of Chicago (▷ 80)
The Palm (▷ 54)

ESSENTIAL CHICAGO WHERE TO EAT BY CUISINE

Top Tips For...

These great suggestions will help you tailor your ideal visit to Chicago, no matter how you choose to spend your time. Each suggestion has a fuller write-up elsewhere in the book.

ENTERTAINING THE KIDS

See the dolphin show at the John G. Shedd Aquarium (▷ 48).
Hit Navy Pier (▷ 64) for the Children's Museum and the new 196-foot high Ferris wheel.
Make the acquaintance of Sue the T. rex at the Field Museum (▷ 46).
Visit the apes at the Lincoln Park Zoo (▷ 62).

OGLING THE ARCHITECTURE

Trek to Frank Lloyd Wright's Home and Studio (▷ 100).
Take the Architecture River Cruise to see the city from the water with the Chicago Architecture Foundation (▷ 24).
Tour the Robie House (▷ 91).
Visit the Glessner House (▷ 87).

The fun of the fair at Navy Pier; dining out; go see a show or visit a comedy club

SAVING MONEY

Venture out into Chicago's neighborhoods, where you'll find budget-friendly and delicious ethnic food (▷ 106).
Ride the El for a budget skyline tour (▷ 26).
Go to the Lincoln Park Zoo (▷ 62) for a second good reason—it's free.
Catch a band outdoors at the Navy Pier beer garden or in Millennium Park's Pritzker Pavilion, also free (▷ 64).

SHOW GOING

Get tickets to the Goodman Theatre (▷ 35) in the Loop.
Spot the celebs on stage at the Steppenwolf Theatre (▷ 78).
Laugh it up at Second City (▷ 67).

DINING WITH A VIEW

Reserve a table at Everest (▷ 37) for western views.

Dine amid the skyline at the Signature Room on the 95th floor in the John Hancock Center (▷ 59).

Go to NoMI, which frames the Historic Water Tower (▷ 112, Park Hyatt Chicago) from its seventh-floor perch.

Regard the Lake Michigan views from this waterfront location at Riva (▷ 80).

Gaze out over Millennium Park from Cindy's, the rooftop bar at the Chicago Athletic Association Hotel (▷ 112).

A NIGHT OUT

Hit the Green Mill Cocktail Lounge (▷ 104) for a live jazz set.

Get the blues at Buddy Guy's Legends (▷ 35).

Check out the local and touring acts on stage at the Metro (▷ 104).

Dance the night away at The Underground Chicago (▷ 36).

SOUVENIR SHOPPING

Enjoy fine dining, live music clubs and shopping for Cubs memorabilia or fashion items

Illinois Artisans Shop (▷ 34) for local artist-made crafts.

Navy Pier shops for trinkets and Chicago Police Department T-shirts (▷ 75).

Hit the Wrigley Field (▷ 101) region for Cubs souvenirs.

FASHION WITH EDGE

Get that California denim look at Current/Elliott (▷ 99).

City Soles (▷ 99) for funky shoes.

Le Thrift Consignment Boutique (▷ 103) for collectors of vintage designer clothing.

P45 (▷ 99) for emerging American designers.

GOING GREEN

Walk the art- and architecture-filled Millennium Park (▷ 50).
Get to Grant Park (▷ 51) in the evening to see Buckingham Fountain's light show.
Visit the greenhouses of the Garfield Park Conservatory (▷ 102).
Tour Lincoln Park, home to a zoo, conservatory, gardens and beaches (▷ 62, 71).

The Gehry-designed bridge in Millennium Park

OUTWARD-BOUND ACTION

Ride a bike along 18 miles (29km) of shoreline parkway (▷ 84).
Get in on a game of sand volleyball at the North Avenue Beach (▷ 66).
Run a 5k race for charity, at one of the lakefront races held each weekend with the Chicago Area Runners Association (CARA).

LOCAL FOOD

Have a hot dog topped with all the fixings at Gold Coast Dogs (▷ panel, 79).
Line up for a high-fat breakfast at Lou Mitchell's (▷ 38).
Devour a slice or two of deep-dish pizza at Gino's East or Pizzeria Uno (▷ panel, 80).
Tuck into Italian classic dishes at Rosebud on Rush (▷ 80) or Maggiano's Little Italy (▷ 80).

Burn off the calories then indulge in pizza or relax at the Peninsula Chicago's luxury spa

HAUT HOTELS

Have high tea in the Palm Court at the Drake (▷ 112).
Be pampered at the spa in the Peninsula hotel (▷ 112).
Ogle the multimillion-dollar art collection at the Park Hyatt Chicago (▷ 112).
Swim beneath shimmering lights in the pool at Langham Hotel Chicago (▷ 112).

Sights	24–31	**THE LOOP**
Walk	32	
Shopping	33–34	
Entertainment and Nightlife	35–36	
Where to Eat	37–38	

Sights	42–51	**MUSEUM CAMPUS**
Walk	52	
Entertainment and Nightlife	53	
Where to Eat	54	

Sights	58–72	**NORTH SIDE**
Walk	73	
Shopping	74–75	
Entertainment and Nightlife	76–78	
Where to Eat	78–80	

Sights	84–91	**SOUTH SIDE**
Walk	92	
Entertainment and Nightlife	93	
Where to Eat	94	

Sights	98–102	**FARTHER AFIELD**
Shopping	103	
Entertainment and Nightlife	104	
Where to Eat	106	

Named for the elevated train that rings the district, the downtown Loop is where Chicago does business. The historic center is also the seat of government and the oldest shopping district in the city.

Sights	24–31
Walk	32
Shopping	33–34
Entertainment and Nightlife	35–36
Where to Eat	37–38

Top 25

TOP 25

Chicago Architecture Foundation River Cruise ▷ 24
Loop Public Sculpture ▷ 25
Riding the El Train ▷ 26
The Rookery ▷ 27
Willis Tower ▷ 28

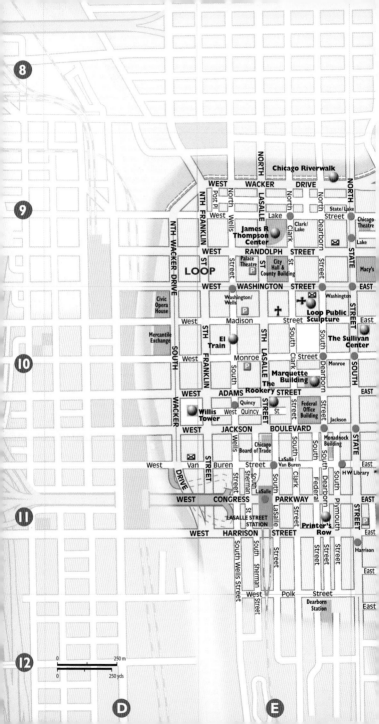

8

9

10

11

12

NORTH

WEST WACKER DRIVE

Chicago Riverwalk

NTH FRANKLIN

North
Post Pl
West
Wells
North
LASALLE
North
Clark
North
Dearborn
State/Lake
Lake
State/Lake

Chicago Theatre

James R Thompson Center

Clark/Lake

WEST RANDOLPH STREET

LOOP

Palace Theatre
ST
Street

City Hall & County Building

Street

STATE

Macy's

WEST WASHINGTON STREET EAST

NTH WACKER DRIVE

Civic Opera House

Mercantile Exchange

Washington/Wells
Madison

STH FRANKLIN

El Train

STH LASALLE

South Street

Washington

Loop Public Sculpture

The Sullivan Center

WASHINGTON STREET

West
South
Monroe
Clark
Street
Dearborn
Monroe

SOUTH STATE

Marquette Building
The Rookery

WEST ADAMS STREET EAST

SOUTH WACKER DRIVE

Willis Tower

Wells
Quincy
West Quincy
St

Quincy
Street
South
South
Federal
Street

Federal Office Building

Street
Jackson

WEST JACKSON BOULEVARD

West
Van Buren

STREET

DRIVE

Chicago Board of Trade

LaSalle/Van Buren
South
South
Clark
South
Dearborn

Monadnock Building

STATE

H W Library

WEST CONGRESS PARKWAY EAST STREET

South Sherman
LaSalle

LASALLE STREET STATION

St
LaSalle
Lasalle
Street
Clark
Street
Federal
Dearborn
Plymouth

Printer's Row

WEST HARRISON STREET East

South Wells Street
South Sherman Street

Street
Street
Street
Street

Harrison

East

West Street
Polk Street
Dearborn Station

East

0   250 m
0   250 yds

D

E

Chicago Architecture Foundation River Cruise

Chicago

EAST WACKER DRIVE

NTH

South North

MICHIGAN

North

Garland

Wabash

Randolph/ Wabash

Ave

Court

WASHINGTON STREET

Madison/ Wabash

Madison

South

Water

North Stetson Avenue

Illinois Center

East Lake Street

American Writers Museum

Prudential Building

EAST RANDOLPH DRIVE

MILLENNIUM STATION

Chicago Cultural Center

Chicago Athenaeum

Street

SOUTH

Lake

Michigan

Wabash

Adams / Wabash

ADAMS ST

MICHIGAN

Orchestra Hall

Avenue

AVENUE

Van Buren St

Congress

Chicago Harbor

CONGRESS PARKWAY

South

Congress Hotel

Harrison Street

Wabash

Museum of Contemporary Photography

Spertus Institute & Museum

Balbo / Avenue

Avenue

East Balbo Drive

Merle Reskin (Blackstone) Theatre

8th Street

Plaza

F

G

The Loop

Chicago Architecture Foundation River Cruise

See the city from the Chicago river aboard a cruise boat

THE BASICS

architecture.org

🔲 F9

✉ 224 Michigan Avenue (board at dock location at Michigan Avenue and Wacker Drive)

☎ 312/922-3432

🕙 10 sailings daily in summer. Closed Dec–Apr

🚇 Brown Line: Randolph

🚌 144, 146, 151

✋ Expensive

HIGHLIGHTS

- Wrigley Building
- Marina City Towers
- 333 W. Wacker Drive
- Chicago River bridges
- Willis Tower
- Tribune Tower

The best of the boat cruises that ply the Chicago River, the Chicago Architecture Foundation's river tours provide knowledgeable narration of 50 distinctive buildings in popular 90-minute outings.

Architectural historians Founded by architects and preservationists in 1966 to preserve the Glessner House on Prairie Avenue, the Chicago Architecture Foundation has grown into the city's most respected leader of design-oriented tours. Arresting buildings loom over passengers gliding by at their bases at water level. Volunteer guides narrate the trip, covering Bertrand Goldberg's 1964 corn-cob-shape Marina City Towers, the triangular, white, tile-clad Wrigley Building erected by the chewing-gum magnate William Wrigley Jr., the black granite art deco tower of the Carbide & Carbon Building from the sons of city planner Daniel Burnham, and the 1922-erected Tribune Tower that, crowned by a series of Gothic flying buttresses inspired by a French cathedral, looks much older. New city landmarks include the shiny Trump Hotel and the Aqua building.

Chicago River In the 17th century Native Americans occupied the banks of the Chicago River where it met Lake Michigan. Over the next centuries as the population grew, wastewater from the river flowed into Lake Michigan, contaminating the city's drinking water. So in 1900 engineers reversed the river's flow away from the lake and into the Sanitary and Ship Canal.

The Flamingo *(left)*;
Monument with
Standing Beast *(right)*

**TOP
25**

Loop Public
Sculpture

**A few blocks in Chicago's Loop district
comprise an outdoor exhibition space
devoted to some of the world's finest
sculptors. It's ideal for those looking for
a cultural self-guided walking tour.**

The collection In 1967 then-mayor Richard
J. Daley dedicated the monumental, untitled
sculpture by Pablo Picasso at Daley Center
Plaza (Dearborn and Washington streets),
considered the first noncommemorative city
sculpture and the start of Chicago's strong
public arts program highlighted by its collection
in the Loop. Across Washington Street, Joan
Miró's depiction of a woman with outstretched
arms faces the Picasso. Marc Chagall's stone
mosaic *The Four Seasons* is at Dearborn and
Monroe streets. Two blocks down at Dearborn
and Adams, Alexander Calder's graceful, neon
orange *Flamingo* contrasts with the dark glass
Federal Center. Jean Dubuffet's white fiberglass
Monument with Standing Beast resides at the
James R. Thompson Center where Clark meets
Randolph Street. And just over the Chicago
River in the West Loop at 600 W. Madison,
Claes Oldenburg created *Batcolumn*, a 100ft
(328m) steel baseball bat.

Chicago's Picasso Chicago architect William
Hartmann convinced Pablo Picasso to create
a sculpture for the city's Civic Center Plaza.
Picasso's untitled work, "a gift to the people of
Chicago," is today part of everyday Loop life,
and skateboarders launch from its sloping base.

THE BASICS

cityofchicago.org/publicart
✛ E10
🚇 Brown, Red, Green
Loop stops
🚌 20, 22

HIGHLIGHTS

● *Untitled* by Pablo Picasso
● *Flamingo* by Alexander
Calder
● *Monument with Standing
Beast* by Jean Dubuffet
● *Chicago* by Joan Miró
● *Batcolumn* by Claes
Oldenburg
● *The Four Seasons* by
Marc Chagall
● *Cloud Gate* (also known
as "the Bean") by Anish
Kapoor
● *Crown Fountain* by
Jaume Plensa
● *Agora* by Magdalena
Abakanowicz

THE LOOP TOP 25

Riding the El Train

The El Train crossing the Chicago River (left); Quincy station (right)

THE BASICS

transitchicago.com

✚ E10

☎ 888/968-7282

🕐 Mon–Sat 5am–1am, Sun 7.16am–12.17am

🚉 Brown Line Loop stops

🚌 29

♿ Inexpensive

HIGHLIGHTS

● Crossing the Chicago River aboard the Brown Line
● Seeing into baseball's Wrigley Field from the Addison stop on the Red Line
● Snaking around the downtown high-rises aboard the Brown Line

FACTS

● Blue Line, largely underground, efficiently connects O'Hare airport to downtown.
● The elevated Orange Line links Midway Airport and downtown.

One of Chicago's most distinctive symbols, the elevated train, El or L for short, provides a commuter's close-up of the city's downtown district as well as its neighborhood backyards.

Tracking history New York erected the first elevated train in 1867, a feat Chicago soon copied, with a flurry of companies devoted to the project. The first line (3.6 miles/5.8km) opened in 1892 and was nicknamed the "Alley L" for running above city-owned alleys, sparing the transit company from securing access privileges from the property owners. Expansion of the El lines was linked to many major events in Chicago history, including the World's Columbian Exposition. Independently owned rail lines agreed to link their services downtown in a "Union Loop" in 1897, the origin of the district's name. Chicago Transit Authority today operates eight color-coded routes over 242 miles (389km) of track.

Brown Line The best line for sightseers, the Brown Line rings the downtown Loop, crosses the Chicago River heading north through the neighborhoods of River North, Lincoln Park, Lakeview and Lincoln Square before terminating at Kimball Street. Board anywhere in the Loop to weave through the high-rises two stories up from street level. Disembark at any stop and, using overhead platform bridges that connect north- and southbound tracks without a transfer fee, return in the opposite direction.

Interior of The Rookery building (left); detail of the exterior of the building (right)

The Rookery

Designed by Daniel Burnham and John Wellborn Root in the 1880s, and later renovated by Frank Lloyd Wright, the Rookery is among Chicago's most admired landmarks.

Birdhouse After the Great Fire of 1871, birds took to roosting in the water-storage building that was temporarily City Hall. It was consequently nicknamed the Rookery. Public feeling dictated that the building that replaced it should formally take on this name. Rising 11 floors, the Rookery was among the tallest buildings in the world on completion and one of the most important early skyscrapers. The thick load-bearing brick-and-granite walls at the base, decorated with Roman, Moorish and Venetian (and several rook) motifs, support upper levels with an iron frame that enabled the structure to be raised higher than previously thought possible. With its masonry exterior and iron interior, the Rookery is considered by architectural historians to be a transitional building in the evolution of the modern skyscraper.

Interior treasures The facade, however, is scant preparation for the interior. The inner court is bathed in incredible natural light entering through a vast domed skylight. Imposing lamps hang above the floor, and Root's intricate ironwork decorates the stairways that climb up to a 360-degree balcony. The white marble, introduced by Frank Lloyd Wright in 1905, increases the sense of space and brightness.

THE BASICS

therookerybuilding.com

➕ E10

✉ 209 S. LaSalle Street

☎ 312/553-6100

🕐 Lobby open during business hours

🚇 Brown, Orange Lines: Quincy

🚌 1, 22, 60, 151

♿ Good

🎫 Free

HIGHLIGHTS

● Light-flooded, glass-roofed inner court
● Ten-story spiral staircase
● Prairie-style light fixtures
● External terra-cotta ornamentation
● Carrara marble walls
● Mosaic tile floors

Willis Tower

HIGHLIGHTS

● Visibility of up to 50 miles (80km) on a clear day
● Standing on The Ledge and daring to look down
● Feeling the building sway
● High-powered telescopes
● Sunset views after 4pm
● Terminals with tower information in several languages

FACTS

● Six robotic window washers mounted on the roof clean all the 16,000 windows.
● Elevators soar 1,600ft (487m) per minute.

Formerly known as the Sears Tower, the Willis Tower rises higher than any other structure in the city. As well as stylish architecture, it has the highest man-made vantage point in the western hemisphere and the vertigo-inducing Ledge.

Built from tubes From 1974 to 1996, the Willis Tower's 110 floors and 1,454ft (443m) height made it the tallest building in the world, rising from the Loop with a distinctive profile of black aluminum and bronze-tinted glass. Architect Bruce Graham, of Skidmore, Owings & Merrill, structured it around nine 75sq ft (7sq m) bundled tubes, which decline in number as the building reaches upward. Aside from increasing the colossal structure's strength, this technique also echoes the stepback, New York skyscraper

Clockwise from top left: People look out over Chicago from the top of the Willis Tower; the view from the Skydeck at the Willis Tower; a 99th-floor event space; a most amazing view from The Ledge

style of the late 1920s. Among the early tasks during the three-year construction was the creation of foundation supports capable of holding a 222,500-ton building. The two roof-top antennae were added in 1982, increasing the building's height by 253ft (77m). Sears, the retail company that commissioned the building of the tower, moved out in 1992.

Seeing for miles The 103rd-floor Skydeck is accessible via a 70-second elevator ride, and reveals an invigorating panorama of the city. An interesting recorded commentary describes the view and landmark buildings. Step out onto The Ledge, a glass-bottomed window extension that lets you look straight down to the city streets and river 1,354ft (412m) below—not recommended if you have a fear of heights.

THE BASICS

theskydeck.com

✛ D10

✉ 233 S. Wacker Drive

☎ 312/875-9696

🕐 Skydeck: Mar–Sep daily 9am–10pm; Oct–Feb 10–8. Last entry 30 minutes before closing. May be closed in high winds

🍴 Various restaurants and cafés

🚇 Brown, Orange Lines: Quincy

🚌 1, 60, 151, 156

♿ Excellent

💲 Moderate

More to See

AMERICAN WRITER'S MUSEUM

americanwritersmuseum.org

Opening in May 2017, this first-of-its-kind national museum celebrates American writers such as Kurt Vonnegut, Mark Twain and Gwendolyn Brooks. Artifacts from the writers' homes will be displayed, as well as interactive, high-tech exhibits that explain each writer's influence on US culture.

➕ F9 ✉ 180 N. Michigan Avenue, 2nd Floor ☎ 312/374-8790 🕐 Tue–Sun 10–4 (till 8pm Thu) 🚇 Brown, Green, Pink, Purple Lines: Randolph/Wabash; Red Line: Lake 🚌 143, 146, 151 ♿ Good 💷 Expensive

CHICAGO CULTURAL CENTER

chicagoculturalcenter.org

The Washington Street entrance leads through hefty bronze doors into the lobby, whose grand staircase is bordered by mosaics set into white marble balustrades. The second floor has the hall and rotunda of the Great Army of the Republic, with Tennessee marble walls and mosaic tile floor, while the floor above holds the Preston Bradley Hall, with a Tiffany-glass dome. The main exhibition hall on the top level features columns that rise to meet a coffered ceiling. The Randolph Street entrance leads to an information center and café.

➕ F9 ✉ 78 E. Washington Street ☎ 312/744-6630 🕐 Mon–Thu 9–7, Fri 9–6, Sat–Sun 10–6 🍴 Café 🚇 Brown, Orange Lines: Madison 🚌 3, 4, 60, 145, 147, 151

CHICAGO RIVERWALK

This developing downtown area along the Chicago River is a lovely place to take a walk or jog, or just sit and watch the boats float past. The area is lined with a plethora of new restaurants and bars, walking paths, floating gardens and a fun splash fountain for kids.

➕ E9 ✉ Banks of Chicago River, beneath Wacker Drive, between State and LaSalle Streets 🚇 Brown, Green, Red, Pink, Purple lines: State/Lake 🚌 151 ♿ Good 💷 Moderate; free Mon

JAMES R. THOMPSON CENTER

cms.il.gov

This distinctive glass-and-steel edifice includes a soaring atrium that is lined with stores, restaurants and cafés; the upper levels house state agencies.

➕ E9 ✉ 100 W. Randolph Street ☎ 312/814-6684 🕐 Mon–Fri 6.30–6 🚇 Blue, Brown, Orange Lines: Clark/Lake 🚌 156 ♿ Good

MARQUETTE BUILDING

marquette.macfound.org

Completed in 1895, it is among the unsung masterpieces of Chicago architecture. It demonstrates the first use of the three-part "Chicago window"—plate glass spans the

Chicago Cultural Center

width between the building's steel supports. Lobby reliefs record the expedition of French Jesuit missionary Jacques Marquette; the entrance doors' panther heads are by Edward Kemeys, also responsible for the lions fronting the Art Institute of Chicago (▷ 44). ➕ E10 ✉ 140 S. Dearborn Street ⏰ Daily 7am–10pm 🚇 Brown, Orange Lines: Quincy

PRINTER'S ROW

The industrial buildings lining Dearborn Street were the core of Chicago's printing industry during the late 19th century. Many are now loft-style apartments, with galleries and restaurants. ➕ E11 ✉ Dearborn Street 🚇 Blue Line: LaSalle; Red Line: Harrison 🚌 22, 62

SPERTUS INSTITUTE & MUSEUM

spertus.edu
Torah scrolls, Hanukkah menorahs and circumcision tools are among the decorative and religious objects spanning 5,000 years featured in the museum's collection of Judaica. The richness of most exhibits contrasts with the somber collection of Holocaust memorabilia. The museum has a kosher café run by chef Wolfgang Puck, a children's center, a gift shop as well as a 400-seat theater. ➕ F11 ✉ 610 S. Michigan Avenue ☎ 312/322-1700 ⏰ Museum: Thu 9–6, Mon–Weds 9–5, Sun 10–5 🚇 Red Line: Harrison 🚌 1, 3, 4, 6, 38, 146 ♿ Good 💰 Moderate

THE SULLIVAN CENTER

thesullivancenter.com
The elaborately decorated exterior of the former Carson Pirie Scott building was created by legendary architect Louis Sullivan over a five-year period beginning in 1899. Vast pieces of glass span the entire width of the building. The Sullivan Center houses retail and office space and The School of the Art Institute of Chicago. ➕ F10 ✉ 1 S. State Street ☎ 312/940-2070 🚇 Blue Line: Madison; Red Line: Monroe 🚌 22, 23, 36, 56, 157 ♿ Good 💰 Free

Marquette Building

Corner entrance to the Sullivan Center

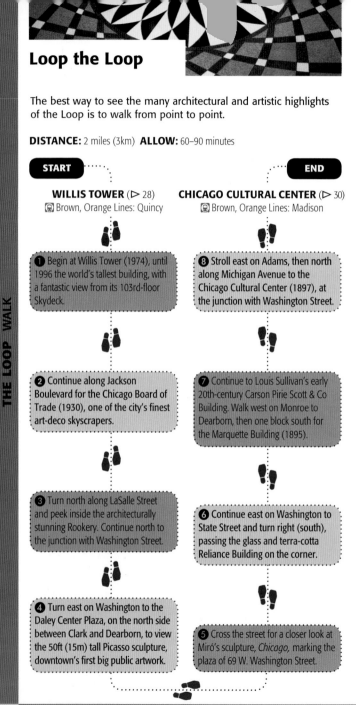

Loop the Loop

The best way to see the many architectural and artistic highlights of the Loop is to walk from point to point.

DISTANCE: 2 miles (3km) **ALLOW:** 60–90 minutes

START

WILLIS TOWER (▷ 28)
🚇 Brown, Orange Lines: Quincy

END

CHICAGO CULTURAL CENTER (▷ 30)
🚇 Brown, Orange Lines: Madison

❶ Begin at Willis Tower (1974), until 1996 the world's tallest building, with a fantastic view from its 103rd-floor Skydeck.

❽ Stroll east on Adams, then north along Michigan Avenue to the Chicago Cultural Center (1897), at the junction with Washington Street.

❷ Continue along Jackson Boulevard for the Chicago Board of Trade (1930), one of the city's finest art-deco skyscrapers.

❼ Continue to Louis Sullivan's early 20th-century Carson Pirie Scott & Co Building. Walk west on Monroe to Dearborn, then one block south for the Marquette Building (1895).

❸ Turn north along LaSalle Street and peek inside the architecturally stunning Rookery. Continue north to the junction with Washington Street.

❻ Continue east on Washington to State Street and turn right (south), passing the glass and terra-cotta Reliance Building on the corner.

❹ Turn east on Washington to the Daley Center Plaza, on the north side between Clark and Dearborn, to view the 50ft (15m) tall Picasso sculpture, downtown's first big public artwork.

❺ Cross the street for a closer look at Miró's sculpture, *Chicago,* marking the plaza of 69 W. Washington Street.

THE LOOP WALK

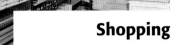

Shopping

ART INSTITUTE OF CHICAGO MUSEUM SHOP

artinstituteshop.org

This outstanding gallery shop features a superb range of fashions including scarves, tote bags and original jewelry, stationery, home furnishings, lamps, sculpture, decorative and fine art, as well as a selection of beautiful books about art and artists.

🗺 F10 ✉ 111 S. Michigan Ave ☎ 312/443-3583 🚇 Blue, Red Lines: Monroe, Jackson 🚌 3, 4, 6, 7, 14, 147, 151

ARTS & ARTISANS

artsartisans.com

For beautiful, one-of-a-kind gifts, visit this family-run store selling fine American crafts, art and jewelry; everything from glass and ceramics to wood carvings. There are three other locations in the downtown area.

🗺 F9 ✉ 35 E. Wacker Drive ☎ 312/578-0126 🚇 Brown, Green, Orange, Pink, Purple Lines: State/Lake 🚌 29, 143, 144, 145, 146, 151

THE ATRIUM MALL

theatriumchicago.com

A range of diverse stores provide an excellent excuse to take a look around the spectacular second floor of this dazzling atrium, a pastiche of glass, marble and steel, with an impressive waterfall.

🗺 E9 ✉ James R. Thompson Center, 100 W. Randolph Street ☎ 312/346-0777 🚇 Blue, Brown, Orange Lines: Clark/Lake 🚌 156

BLICK ART MATERIALS

dickblick.com

Art supply store Blick stocks everything from oil paints to sculptor's clay. Sketchpads and kids' projects may appeal to travelers.

🗺 F10 ✉ 42 S. State Street ☎ 312/920-0300 🚇 Red Line: Madison 🚌 29

BOOKSAMILLION

booksamillion.com

There could well be over a million books, mostly mainstream titles on diverse subjects, amid these tightly stacked shelves.

🗺 E10 ✉ 144 S. Clark Street ☎ 312/857-0613 🚇 Blue, Red Lines: Washington 🚌 22, 24

CHICAGO ARCHITECTURE FOUNDATION

architecture.org

Exemplary source of books on architecture, as well as clever, colorful gifts that make tasteful souvenirs.

🗺 F11 ✉ 224 S. Michigan Avenue ☎ 312/922-3432 🚇 Brown, Orange Lines: Adams 🚌 3, 4, 6, 38

DYLAN'S CANDY BAR

dylanscandybar.com/info/chicago.html

The Chicago outpost of this popular New York City candy store offers two floors packed with colorful candy. The place has a Willy Wonka feel to it, with retro candies plus their best-selling oversized whirly pop lollipops and chocolate bars. Be sure to check out the fun display of celebrities' favorite candies.

🗺 F8 ✉ 445 N. Michigan Ave ☎ 312/702-2247 🚇 Red Line: Grand 🚌 143, 146, 151

PRINTER'S ROW LIT FEST

To celebrate this district's history in all things print production, Chicago's annual Printer's Row Lit Fest (printersrowlitfest.org), held over a weekend in early June, lures new, used and antiques booksellers to temporary shops that are erected under tents lining South Dearborn between Congress and Polk. Event programs include author readings and signings, and discussions.

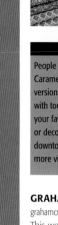
GARRETT POPCORN

People line up for blocks to buy their CaramelCrisp, CheeseCorn and butter versions of this popcorn, which is popular with tourists and celebrities. Mix a few of your favorite types together in a bag, box or decorative tin. They have eight locations downtown including Navy Pier. To find out more visit garrettpopcorn.com.

GRAHAM CRACKERS COMICS

grahamcrackers.com

This well-stocked comic-book store appeals to the area's college students and comic aficionados.

F10 ⊠ 77 E. Madison Street ☎ 312/629-1810 Red Line: Madison 29

ILLINOIS ARTISANS SHOP

museum.state.il.us

On the second floor of the James R. Thompson Center, Illinois Artisans Shop showcases the work of artists around the state working in jewelry, ceramics, wood and textiles with semiannual exhibits of fine art.

E9 ⊠ James R. Thompson Center, 100 W. Randolph Street ☎ 312/814-5321 Blue, Brown, Orange Lines: Clark/Lake 156

THE JEWELER'S CENTER

jewelerscenter.com

Jewelry and other related products are sold in more than 180 outlets over 13 floors; if you can't find what you're looking for here, you never will.

F10 ⊠ 5 S. Wabash Avenue ☎ 312/424-2664 Brown, Orange Lines: Madison 38

MACY'S

visitmacyschicago.com

Once home to the beloved Marshall Field's department store, the New York-based Macy's chain has retained many of the old store's famous features, including the century-old green clock that hangs outside. Inside, the store sells clothing, home goods and jewelry. It also houses several restaurants, such as the legendary Walnut Room.

F10 ⊠ 111 N. State Street ☎ 312/781-4483 Blue, Red Lines: Washington 6, 11, 29, 36, 44, 62, 146

POSTER PLUS

posterplus.com

Head here for historic posters, mostly celebrating landmarks in Chicago and US history, though many are attractive reprints rather than originals.

F11 ⊠ 30 E. Adams Street, Suite 1150 ☎ 312/461-9277 Brown, Orange Lines: Adams 3, 4, 6, 38

SEPHORA MICHIGAN AVENUE

sephora.com/stores/chicago-michigan-ave

While this cosmetics chain has more than 400 stores, this new location is its first "Beauty TIP" (Teach, Inspire, Play) store in the Midwest. Customers are invited to experiment with most of their 13,000 products and ask questions or get advice at the Beauty Bar and Skincare Studio. Register in advance online for a free beauty class.

F8 ⊠ 605 N. Michigan Ave ☎ 312/649-9343 Red Line: Grand 143, 146, 151

SYD JEROME

sydjerome.com

Esquire magazine rated this upscale men's store "Best in Class" for its range of impeccably stylish and elegant fashions coming from the likes of Armani, Hickey Freeman and Jhane Barnes.

E10 ⊠ 2 N. LaSalle Street ☎ 312/346-0333 Brown, Orange, Pink, Purple Lines: Washington/Wells 134, 135, 136, 156

Entertainment and Nightlife

AUDITORIUM THEATRE
auditoriumtheatre.org
Designed by the revered Adler & Sullivan, the marvelously renovated Auditorium Building is a fine venue for dance, music and drama productions.
➕ F11 ✉ 50 E. Congress Parkway
☎ 312/922-2110 🚇 Red Line: Harrison
🚌 6, 145, 146, 147, 151

BUDDY GUY'S LEGENDS
buddyguy.com
Co-owner and famed blues guitarist Buddy Guy presents outstanding blues acts, including internationally known names and local rising stars.
➕ F11 ✉ 700 S. Wabash Avenue
☎ 312/427-1190 🚇 Red Line: Harrison
🚌 12

CADILLAC PALACE THEATRE
broadwayinchicago.com
One of Chicago's major theaters along Randolph Street, comprising the Loop's theater district, the Cadillac Palace is often booked by big Broadway touring companies.
➕ E9 ✉ 151 W. Randolph Street
☎ 312/977-1700 🚇 Brown, Orange Lines: Washington 🚌 156

CHICAGO THEATRE
thechicagotheatre.com
The 3,600-seat, French baroque-style Chicago Theatre, with the classic vertical C-H-I-C-A-G-O spelled out on the marquee, hosts concert tours in rock, jazz, hip-hop and ballet, as well as limited-run theater productions.
➕ F9 ✉ 175 N. State Street ☎ 800/745-3000 🚇 Red Line: Lake 🚌 29

CIVIC OPERA HOUSE
civicoperahouse.com
The distinguished Lyric Opera of Chicago company perform from late September to the end of March at this art-deco auditorium (also one of the main dance venues). Seats are sometimes available at the box office on the day of the performance.
➕ D10 ✉ 20 N. Wacker Drive ☎ 312/419-0033 🚇 Brown, Orange Lines: Madison/Wells 🚌 129

GENE SISKEL FILM CENTER
siskelfilmcenter.org
The School of the Arts Institute of Chicago runs this ambitious cinema named for a former, highly influential film critic. Two screens show independent, foreign and vintage films in repertory, the type of arty fare you won't find at the normal Cineplex.
➕ F9 ✉ 164 N. State Street ☎ 312/846-2800 🚇 Red Line: Lake 🚌 29

GOODMAN THEATRE
goodmantheatre.org
The Goodman hosts some of the best drama in the city, including both classics and cutting-edge contemporary productions. Well-known actors including Brian Dennehy and Marcia Gay Harden have performed here and playwrights August Wilson and Arthur Miller debuted plays here.
➕ E9 ✉ 170 N. Dearborn Street
☎ 312/443-3800 🚇 Red Line: Washington
🚌 22, 24, 36, 62

COMEDY SHOWS
Entertaining Chicago theatergoers for years. *Late Nite Catechism/Bible* Bingo (✉ Royal George Theater, 1641 N. Halsted ☎ 312/988-9000) is a hilarious, interactive one-woman show on Thursday and Saturday. Audience members actually play games of bingo.

THE LIVING ROOM

whotels.com

The style-focused W Chicago City Center makes a lounge of its historic lobby, wth a DJ on the mezzanine playing to patrons arrayed on sofas.

➕ E10 ✉ 172 W. Adams Street
☎ 312/332-1200 🚇 Brown Line: Quincy
🚌 156

ORIENTAL THEATER

broadwayinchicago.com

This ornate theater presents first-rate shows in its fine performance space.

➕ E9 ✉ 24 W. Randolph Street
☎ 312/902-1400 🚇 Red, Brown, Green, Orange Lines: Lake 🚌 156

PRIVATEBANK THEATRE

broadwayinchicago.com

This handsome place is a rare reminder that theater once thrived in the Loop. It is best known for its musicals.

➕ F10 ✉ 18 W. Monroe Street ☎ 312/341-2310 🚇 Brown, Orange Lines: Madison/Wells 🚌 29

REDHEAD PIANO BAR

theredheadpianobar.com

Here, sit and listen, or step up near the piano to sing along with other patrons. The walls are lined with sheet music and photos of stars of yesteryear.

➕ E8 ✉ 16 W. Ontario ☎ 312/640-1000
🚇 Red Line: Grand 🚌 125, 65

HALF-PRICE TICKETS

Hot Tix (✉ 72 E. Randolph Street or 108 N. State Street) offers half-price tickets for many of the day's theater events. A website (hottix.org) lists the day's performances. Full-price advance tickets are also available from Hot Tix, as well as from Ticketmaster (☎ 312/559-1212).

ROOF ON THE WIT

roofonthewit.com

Often ranked as one of the world's best rooftop bars, the ROOF is known for its far-reaching views of downtown Chicago. Such is its popularity that no reservations are taken, and lines can be long, especially on weekends, as its house and celeb DJs mix current hits with party rock.

➕ F9 ✉ 201 N. State Street ☎ 312/239-9502 🚇 Red Line: Lake 🚌 143, 144, 145, 146

SYMPHONY CENTER

cso.org

From September to May the renowned Chicago Symphony Orchestra (CSO) is in residence in this sumptuous Greek Revival hall, built in 1904. Tickets are sold early, but some may be available on the day of performance. The Civic Orchestra of Chicago, a training orchestra, gives free concerts and there is an annual jazz series here.

➕ F10 ✉ 220 S. Michigan Avenue
☎ 312/294-3000 🚇 Brown, Orange Lines: Adams 🚌 1, 3, 4, 6, 7, 38, 60

UNDERGOUND

theundergroundchicago.com

Dance into the wee hours and sip cool cocktails at this sexy, late-night club featuring some of the country's top DJs. Celebrities often drop in (Justin Bieber, Emmy Rossum and Nick Jonas were recent guests) and mingle with the nicely dressed crowd. The club has two spaces—a high-energy, modern dance club area, and an old-school, upscale lounge with plush seating. Complimentary cookies are given out each night at 1am.

➕ D8 ✉ 56 W. Illinois ☎ 312/644-7600
🚇 Red Line: Grand 🚌 156

Where to Eat

THE LOOP WHERE TO EAT

<table>
<tr><td colspan="2">PRICES</td></tr>
</table>

PRICES

Prices are approximate, based on a
3-course meal for one person.

$$$$	over $50
$$$	$31–$50
$$	$16–$30
$	up to $15

312 CHICAGO ($$$)

312chicago.com

One of the best Italian specialists in the
Loop, 312 Chicago adjoins the Allegro
Hotel and, like others near the theater
district, requires a reservation.

🔲 E9 ✉ 136 N. LaSalle Street ☎ 312/696-
2420 🕐 Daily breakfast, lunch and dinner;
Sat–Sun brunch 🚇 Brown, Orange Lines:
Washington 🚌 129

ATWOOD ($$)

atwoodrestaurant.com

Dine on foods such as maple-cured
pork chops and chicken pot pie. Café
staples including salads and soups
lighten up the lunch fare at this window-
wrapped restaurant.

🔲 E9 ✉ 1 W. Washington Street
☎ 312/368-1900 🕐 Daily breakfast, lunch
and dinner 🚇 Red Line: Washington 🚌 29

BAVETTE'S BAR & BOEUF ($$$)

bavetteschicago.comm

One of Chicago's best steak houses, this
dinner-only, speakeasy-styled restaurant
also impresses with its seafood, the
international wines and strong cocktails.

🔲 E9 ✉ 218 W. Kinzie Street ☎ 312/624-
8154 🕐 Daily dinner only 🚇 Purple, Brown
Lines: Merchandise Mart 🚌 29

THE BERGHOFF ($$)

theberghoff.com

A direct descendant of one of Chicago's
most fondly remembered restaurants,
the historic Berghoff serves classic
German fare such as *sauerbraten* and
Wiener schnitzel in an Old World-
inspired room with stained-glass
accents. The café makes a great stop
for lunchtime sandwiches.

🔲 E10 ✉ 17 W. Adams Street ☎ 312/427-
3170 🚇 Red Line: Jackson 🚌 29

EVEREST ($$$$)

everestrestaurant.com

This 40th-floor top-notch restaurant that
commands far-reaching views—beloved
of financial wheeler-dealers—offers an
inspiring look at chef Jean Joho's native
Alsace. The restaurant's Loop location,
prices and standards of cooking are all
breathtakingly high.

🔲 E10 ✉ 440 S. LaSalle Street ☎ 312/663-
8920 🕐 Dinner only; closed Sun, Mon
🚇 Blue Line: LaSalle 🚌 22

EXCHEQUER ($$)

exchequerpub.com

Friendly family-run place that's always
busy thanks to its great ribs, pizza and
classic American dishes, like the Bistro
Burger. Lots of good draught beers too.

🔲 F10 ✉ 226 S. Wabash Avenue
☎ 312/939-5633 🕐 Daily lunch and dinner
🚇 Brown, Green, Orange, Pink, Purple Lines:
Adams/ Wabash 🚌 7, 126, 151

THE ITALIAN VILLAGE
RESTAURANTS ($$–$$$$)

italianvillage-chicago.com

Three Italians in one building: The
expensive and smart Vivere, the mid-
priced and seafood-focused La Cantina
and the good-value, the Village.

🔲 E10 ✉ 71 W. Monroe Street ☎ 312/332-
7005 🕐 Vivere: Mon–Fri lunch, Sat–Sun
dinner; La Cantina: Tue–Sat dinner only; The
Village: daily lunch and dinner 🚇 Red Line:
Monroe 🚌 29

LOU MITCHELL'S ($)

loumitchellsrestaurant.com

Longstanding Chicago diner serves omelets and home-baked pastries.

F9 ✉ 565 W. Jackson Boulevard ☎ 312/939-3111 🕐 Breakfast and lunch only 🚇 Brown, Orange Lines: Quincy 🚌 126

PETTERINO'S ($$$)

petterinos.com

This is a supper-club style restaurant that specializes in steaks and seafood. It is a popular pre-theater stop.

E9 ✉ 150 N. Dearborn Street ☎ 312/422-0150 🕐 Daily lunch and dinner 🚇 Brown, Orange Lines: Clark/Lake 🚌 156

PORTILLO'S HOT DOGS & BARNELLI'S SALAD BOWL ($)

portillos.com

This is the place for a real Chicago hot dog or Italian beef sandwich. Order at the counter and then find a seat in the memorabilia-covered dining area.

E8 ✉ 100 W. Ontario Street ☎ 312/587-8910 🕐 Daily lunch and dinner 🚇 Red Line: Grand 🚌 156

RPM ITALIAN ($$$)

rpmrestaurants.com/rpmitalian/chicago/

Homemade pastas, plus classic Italian food with a contemporary twist are served in this sleek yet unpretentious setting.

F10 ✉ 52 W. Illinois ☎ 312/222-1888 🕐 Mon–Sat dinner, Sun lunch and dinner 🚇 Red Line: Grand 🚌 156

RUSSIAN TEA TIME ($$)

russianteatime.com

Balalaika music plays in this wood-covered room with red leather booths. Hearty foods are on the menu, but so is caviar, roast pheasant, iced vodka and other Russian specialties.

F10 ✉ 77 E. Adams Street ☎ 312/360-0000 🕐 Daily lunch, dinner and Afternoon Tea 🚇 Brown, Orange Lines: Adams 🚌 1, 7, 60, 126, 151

SEVEN ON STATE ($)

On the seventh floor of Macy's, this upscale food court includes Mexican and Asian kiosks, as well as soups, salads and sandwiches.

F9 ✉ 111 N. State Street ☎ 312/781-3693 🕐 Mon–Sat 10–9, Sun 11–7 🚇 Red Line: Washington 🚌 29

SOUTH WATER KITCHEN ($$$)

southwaterkitchen.com

Inside the Hotel Monaco, South Water Kitchen is all about classic American fare and, on Friday, fried fish. Gluten free food is also availablle.

F9 ✉ 225 N. Wabash Avenue ☎ 312/236-9300 🕐 Daily dinner; Mon–Fri breakfast and lunch, Sat–Sun brunch 🚇 Red Line: Lake; Brown, Green, Orange Lines: State 🚌 29

TRATTORIA NO. 10 ($$$)

trattoriaten.com

This subterranean pasta specialist near theaters draws sell-out crowds and reservations are required.

E9 ✉ 10 N. Dearborn Street ☎ 312/984-1718 🕐 No lunch Sat; closed Sun 🚇 Blue Line: Washington 🚌 29

FOR VEGETARIANS

Most Chinese, Thai and Vietnamese restaurants offer meat-free versions of their staples, as do Indian eateries; Italian restaurants are another likely possibility. Among the almost exclusively vegetarian restaurants try Chicago Diner (✉ 3411 N. Halsted Street ☎ 773/935-6696) and Dharma Garden Thai (✉ 3109 W. Irving Park Road ☎ 773/588-9140).

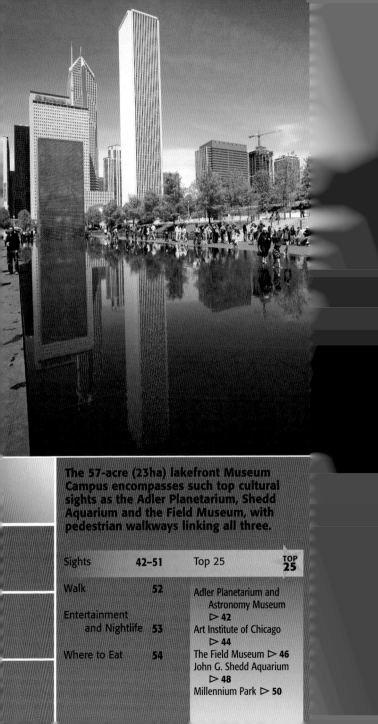

The 57-acre (23ha) lakefront Museum Campus encompasses such top cultural sights as the Adler Planetarium, Shedd Aquarium and the Field Museum, with pedestrian walkways linking all three.

Sights	42–51	Top 25	TOP 25
Walk	52		
		Adler Planetarium and Astronomy Museum ▷ 42	
Entertainment and Nightlife	53	Art Institute of Chicago ▷ 44	
Where to Eat	54	The Field Museum ▷ 46	
		John G. Shedd Aquarium ▷ 48	
		Millennium Park ▷ 50	

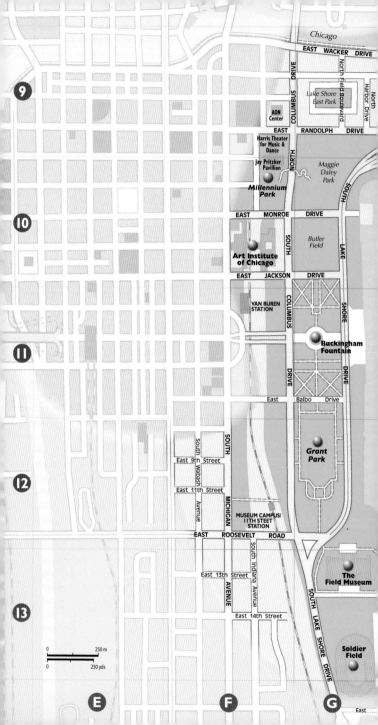

Chicago

EAST WACKER DRIVE

North Harbor Drive

North Field Boulevard

DRIVE

COLUMBUS

Lake Shore East Park

AON Center

EAST RANDOLPH DRIVE

Harris Theater for Music & Dance

Jay Pritzker Pavilion

NORTH

Maggie Daley Park

Millennium Park

EAST MONROE DRIVE

SOUTH

Butler Field

LAKE

Art Institute of Chicago

EAST JACKSON DRIVE

VAN BUREN STATION

COLUMBUS

SHORE

Buckingham Fountain

DRIVE

East Balbo Drive

Grant Park

DRIVE

South Wabash

South Michigan Avenue

East 9th Street

East 11th Street

MUSEUM CAMPUS/ 11TH STEET STATION

EAST ROOSEVELT ROAD

The Field Museum

South Indiana Avenue

East 13th Street

AVENUE

SOUTH LAKE SHORE DRIVE

East 14th Street

Soldier Field

0   250 m
0   250 yds

9

10

11

12

13

E   F   G

East

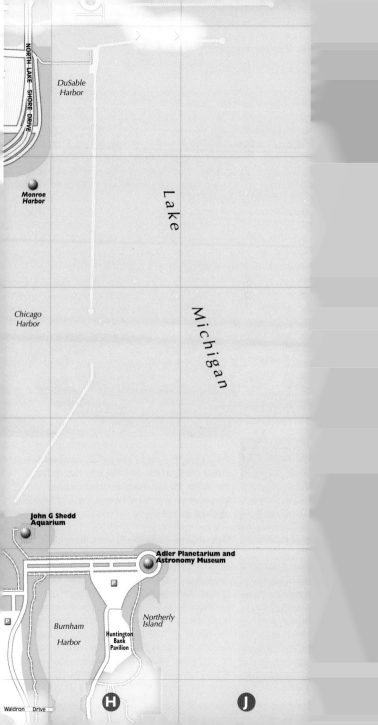

NORTH LAKE SHORE DRIVE

DuSable
Harbor

Monroe
Harbor

Lake

Michigan

Chicago
Harbor

John G Shedd
Aquarium

Adler Planetarium and
Astronomy Museum

Burnham
Harbor

Huntington
Bank
Pavilion

Northerly
Island

Waldron Drive

H

J

Adler Planetarium and Astronomy Museum

HIGHLIGHTS

- Sky Theater
- Definiti Space Theater
- Mission Moon
- Atwood Sphere
- Space Visualization Laboratory

TIPS

- Be prepared to pay the two-show entry fee to experience the Adler in full.
- Visitors are drawn to the razzle dazzle of the Definiti Space Theater, but the Sky Theater's re-creation of the sky is more educational.

Projecting the night sky on an overhead dome (68ft/21m), Sky Theater has helped the Adler Planetarium and Astronomy Museum to win local hearts since it opened in 1930.

Skywatching Max Adler, a Sears Roebuck executive, realized his ambition to put the wonders of the cosmos within the reach of ordinary people when he provided the money to have the western hemisphere's first modern planetarium built in Chicago. The planetarium holds one of the world's major astronomical collections. This landmark building is a dodeca-hedron in rainbow granite, decorated with signs of the zodiac and topped by a lead-covered copper dome. The fascinating Sky Theater examines constellations and planets as they

Clockwise from left: The Adler Planetarium with the city in the background; the audience admires Jupiter in the Definiti Space Theater; the austere exterior of the Adler Planetarium belies the amazing sights within; a solar system exhibit

appear in the current night sky, projected onto an overhead dome. The Definiti Space Theater uses digital technology and three-dimensional graphics to journey into space. Adler After Dark is exclusively for adults aged 21 and over. This evening program offers unlimited shows and open access every third Thursday of the month.

Finding space Planet Explorers is a space exploration experience for kids. Other areas are devoted to how changing perceptions of the universe affected human culture, and the practicalities of exploring space, with items from manned exploration and samples of moon and Martian rock. Mission Moon lets visitors experience America's first steps into space through the eyes of NASA captain James Lovell Jr. and his family.

THE BASICS

adlerplanetarium.org

✚ H13

✉ 1300 S. Lake Shore Drive

☎ 312/322-7827

🕐 Daily 9.30–4.30. Closed Thanksgiving, Dec 25. Check for special weekend and evening hours and events

🍽 Cafeteria

Ⓜ Orange Line: Roosevelt

🚆 Roosevelt Road

🚌 146

♿ Good

💲 Moderate–Expensive

Art Institute of Chicago

HIGHLIGHTS

● *Time Transfixed*, René Magritte
● *A Sunday on La Grande Jatte*, Georges Seurat
● *Paris Street; Rainy Day*, Gustave Caillebotte
● *Mother and Child*, Picasso
● *Two Sisters (on the Terrace)*, Renoir
● *American Gothic*, Grant Wood
● *Nighthawks*, Hopper

TIPS

● Visit on a weekday (weekends are very busy).
● If time-pressed, head directly for the Impressionist galleries.

Housed in a building erected for the World's Columbian Exposition in 1893, the Art Institute has an acclaimed collection of Impressionist paintings. But its splendid galleries showcase a lot more, from arms and armor to the original trading room of the Stock Exchange.

Masterworks The celebrated *American Gothic* by Grant Wood and Edward Hopper's moody *Nighthawks* are among the highlights of the American collections. The Impressionist galleries and European art are on level 2. No work receives greater notice and admiration than Georges Seurat's expansive *A Sunday on La Grande Jatte*, a pointillist masterpiece. Seminal works in adjacent galleries include haystacks by Claude Monet, dancers by Edgar Degas, a

self-portrait on cardboard by Vincent van Gogh and the vibrant *Paris Street; Rainy Day* by Gustave Caillebotte. The stunning new Modern Wing houses 20th- and 21st-century modern and contemporary art.

Curiosities Everything from Chinese ceramics to Guatemalan textiles has a niche on the first floor. Leave time for the stunning 1898 Trading Room of the Chicago Stock Exchange, designed by Louis Sullivan and reconstructed here. The lower level photography gallery exhibits select works from its comprehensive collection and the Thorne Miniature Rooms re-create 68 historic settings in 1-inch-to-1-foot (2.5cm-to-30cm) scale. There are also regular changing exhibitions from all over the world, and a museum shop.

THE BASICS

artic.edu

🞢 F10

✉ 111 S. Michigan Avenue

☎ 312/443-3600

🕐 Mon–Wed, Fri 10.30–5, Thu 10.30–8, Sat–Sun 10–5

🍴 Cafés

🚇 Brown, Orange Lines: Adams

🚌 3, 4, 60, 145, 147, 151

♿ Good

💵 Expensive; free to Illinois residents Thu 5–8

❓ Free tours daily via App

The Field Museum

HIGHLIGHTS

● Sue
● "Traveling the Pacific"
● Dinosaur Hall
● Crown Family PlayLab
● Pawnee earth lodge
● The Ancient Americas
● 3-D movies
● Evolving planet

TIPS

● This vast museum requires a game plan on entry, and the menu of options often includes blockbuster touring exhibitions.
● In fair weather have a picnic on the front or back steps of the museum.

One of the world's great natural history museums, the Field displays wonderful exhibits drawn from all corners of the globe. After a strenuous round of viewing, ponder the fact that only around one percent of the museum's 20 million artifacts is on display.

The building The museum was completed in 1920, its cavernous galleries providing a home for a collection originally assembled for Chicago's 1893 World's Columbian Exposition. With its porticoes, columns and beaux-arts decoration, the imposing design sits rather uneasily with the needs of a modern museum, and sometimes the many rooms of exhibits from myriad eras and cultures can make for jumbled viewing. But the building's many

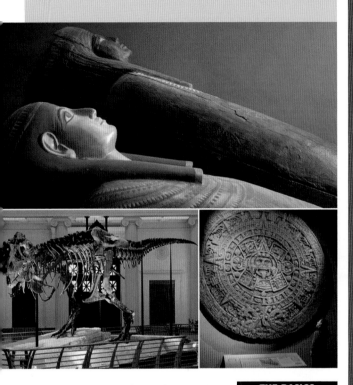

Clockwise from left: stone columns mark the entrance to the museum; Egyptian mummy masks; a magnificent sunstone; an Albertosaurus on display in the Stanley Field Hall

sequestered galleries make an adventure of exploring the dinosaur galleries, the taxidermy-mad World of Mammals, the life of an underground bug and corners of investigation.

Great exhibits The outstanding sections include the dinosaur exhibits in which Sue, the most complete *Tyrannosaurus rex* ever found, takes pride of place in the entrance hall; major ancient Egyptian artifacts, spanning 5000BC to AD300, arranged in and around the life-size, re-created tomb of a 5th-dynasty pharaoh; and "Traveling the Pacific," a powerful examination of cultural and spiritual life in Pacific cultures and the threats posed by the Western world's encroachment. Also noteworthy are the Native American displays and the gem collection, which includes pieces by Tiffany & Co.

THE BASICS

fieldmuseum.org

➕ G13

✉ 1400 S. Lake Shore Drive

☎ 312/922-9410

🕐 Daily 9–5

🍴 The Field Bistro and Explorer Cafe

Ⓢ Orange Line: Roosevelt

🚏 Roosevelt Road

🚌 146

♿ Good

💰 Expensive

John G. Shedd Aquarium

HIGHLIGHTS

- Pacific white-sided dolphins
- Beluga whales
- Sea otters
- Sea anemones
- Penguins
- Turtles
- Sharks

Chicago's "Ocean-by-the-Lake" is the world's largest indoor aquarium, enhanced by a state-of-the-art ocean-arium where dolphins and whales show off typical behaviors, and a Philippine reef exhibit showcasing sharks.

Aquarium A re-created Caribbean coral reef at the core of this imposing Greek-style building is home to barracuda, moray eels, nurse sharks and other creatures, who are fed several times daily by a team of microphone-equipped divers who describe the creatures, their habits and their habitat. Around the reef, denizens of the deep waters of the world occupy geographically arranged tanks. Watch out for the false-eye flashlight fish, born with the piscine equivalent of a flashlight.

Clockwise from left: dolphins delight their onlookers; the handsome stone entrance; a turtle enjoys a swim; a curious Gentoo penguin

JOHN G. SHEDD AQUARIUM

WELCOME

Oceanarium Dolphins and beluga whales are the star attractions here. Several times daily, the dolphins display natural skills such as "spy-hopping," when a dolphin raises itself onto its tail, in a schmaltzy amphitheater show called "Fantasea." Winding nature trails lead to the lower-level windows that provide an under-water view of the dolphins and whales. You also see a colony of penguins and sea otters. Descend by elevator to the Wild Reef to see fascinating tropical creatures such as sea drag-ons, whiptail rays and lionfish. Only a 0.25-inch (0.6cm) thick window separates visitors from 30 sharks swimming in a massive floor-to-ceiling tank, which re-creates a reef in the Philippines. Organized activities also go on in the evenings and the "Asleep with the Fishes" sleepovers are especially popular with children.

THE BASICS

sheddaquarium.org

➕ G12

✉ 1200 S. Lake Shore Drive

☎ 312/939-2438

🕐 Daily 9–6 Jun–Aug; Mon–Fri 9–5 Sep–May. Last entry 45 minutes before closing

🍴 Soundings Restaurant; Deep Ocean Café; snacks at Bubble Net Food Court

🚇 Orange Line: Roosevelt

🚉 Roosevelt Road

🚌 146

🍴 Excellent

♿ Expensive; free on Community Discount Days (see website); some exhib-its at reduced fee; Asleep with the Fishes expensive

Millennium Park

Jay Pritzker Pavilion (left) and Cloud Gate *by Anish Kapoor (right)*

THE BASICS

millenniumpark.org
🔁 F10
✉ 201 E. Randolph Drive
☎ 312/742-1168
🍴 Park Grill, snack shop
🚇 Brown, Green, Orange Lines: Randolph
🚌 127, 144, 146, 151
♿ Good
✋ Free

HIGHLIGHTS

● Jay Pritzker Pavilion
● *Cloud Gate*, (The Bean) Anish Kapoor
● The Crown Fountain
● BP Bridge
● Maggie Daley Park
● Ice-skating rink
● Chase Promenade
● Boeing Galleries sculptures

This art-and-architecture-filled park is Chicago's crown jewel. Start by snapping "The Bean," the park's unusual sculpture, then stroll around and enjoy the gardens, water-play area and frequent concerts.

Cutting-edge culture City planner Daniel Burnham put his stamp on Grant Park in the early 1900s, giving the city an apron of green at its front door. Millennium Park updates the civic respite concept with new landmarks by design-world greats including architect Frank Gehry, who brought his signature swooping-titanium style to the erection of the park's central theater, the Jay Pritzker Pavilion. Gehry also designed the winding bridge (308yd/281m) that leads parkgoers lakeward. The Crown Fountain's twin glass towers (50ft/15m) project video images of a cross section of Chicagoans in portrait, while in summer children run beneath the water jets. Plazas, promenades, gardens and a restaurant with a large outdoor café in summer.

The Bean Briton Anish Kapoor created the 110-ton elliptical sculpture *Cloud Gate*, known locally as "the Bean." Its highly polished surface bends and warps the surrounding skyline in reflection, a sight that commonly attracts photographers. Briefly, the city tried to block people from capturing its image, claiming copyright infringement. Public uproar duly followed and officials relented, though the city maintains that anyone seeking to publish images of the Bean needs the permission of the artist.

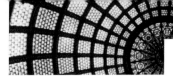

More to See

BUCKINGHAM FOUNTAIN
Among the features of Grant Park is the 1926 Buckingham Fountain. Designed by Edward H. Bennett, it is notable for its choreographed colorful lights dancing on the 1.5 million gallons (6.8 million liters) of water that are pumped daily.
🔲 G11 ✉ Grant Park ⏱ Apr to mid-Oct 8am–11pm

GRANT PARK
Planned by Daniel Burnham in 1909 as the centerpiece of a series of lakefront parks, Grant Park is a major festival venue that has seen everything from a violence-marred 1968 anti-Vietnam War demonstration to a papal Mass in 1979. Grant Park is essentially a succession of lawns crisscrossed by walkways and split in two by busy Lake Shore Drive. Bordered by the high-rises of the Loop and the expanses of Lake Michigan, Grant Park never lets you forget that you are in Chicago. Its Petrillo Music Shell provides a setting for summer concerts.

🔲 G12 ✉ Bordered by S. Michigan Avenue, E. Randolph Drive, E. Roosevelt Road and Lake Michigan ☎ Petrillo Music Shell concert information: 312/742-4763 ⏱ Visit during daylight hours only, except for special evening events 🚇 Brown, Orange Lines: Randolph, Madison or Adams 🚌 3, 4, 6, 38, 60, 145, 146, 147, 151, 157

MONROE HARBOR
Some 1,000 boats moor here, just across Lake Shore Drive from Grant Park, providing a picturesque foreground for a lakefront stroll.
🔲 G10 ✉ Grant Park

SOLDIER FIELD
soldierfield.net
The original 1924 colonnaded Greek Revival stadium is home to football's Chicago Bears. A 2003 addition resembling a glass-and-steel spaceship set down within the classic arcade wall updated the services of the stadium.
🔲 G13 ✉ 1410 S. Museum Drive ☎ 312/235-7000 🚇 Red Line: Roosevelt 🚌 12, 127

MUSEUM CAMPUS MORE TO SEE

Buckingham Fountain

A Walk in the Park

A stroll through Chicago's front yard takes you to and past some of the city's best cultural attractions and mostly away from car traffic.

DISTANCE: Around 2 miles (3km) **ALLOW:** 90 minutes without museum stops

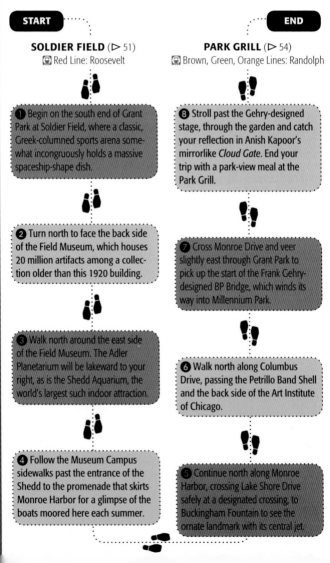

START

SOLDIER FIELD (▷ 51)
🚇 Red Line: Roosevelt

END

PARK GRILL (▷ 54)
🚇 Brown, Green, Orange Lines: Randolph

❶ Begin on the south end of Grant Park at Soldier Field, where a classic, Greek-columned sports arena somewhat incongruously holds a massive spaceship-shape dish.

❷ Turn north to face the back side of the Field Museum, which houses 20 million artifacts among a collection older than this 1920 building.

❸ Walk north around the east side of the Field Museum. The Adler Planetarium will be lakeward to your right, as is the Shedd Aquarium, the world's largest such indoor attraction.

❹ Follow the Museum Campus sidewalks past the entrance of the Shedd to the promenade that skirts Monroe Harbor for a glimpse of the boats moored here each summer.

❽ Stroll past the Gehry-designed stage, through the garden and catch your reflection in Anish Kapoor's mirrorlike *Cloud Gate*. End your trip with a park-view meal at the Park Grill.

❼ Cross Monroe Drive and veer slightly east through Grant Park to pick up the start of the Frank Gehry-designed BP Bridge, which winds its way into Millennium Park.

❻ Walk north along Columbus Drive, passing the Petrillo Band Shell and the back side of the Art Institute of Chicago.

❺ Continue north along Monroe Harbor, crossing Lake Shore Drive safely at a designated crossing, to Buckingham Fountain to see the ornate landmark with its central jet.

Entertainment and Nightlife

CHICAGO SUMMER DANCE

cityofchicago.org

Every weekend throughout the summer, the city of Chicago hosts a free dance party in the Spirit of Music Garden in Grant Park, with live bands and dance lessons. Organizers set down a massive dance floor, where people are invited to dance to swing or salsa or whatever the night's theme may be. All dance levels are welcome.

🔲 G12 ✉ Grant Park (▷ 51)

CINDY'S

cindysrooftopbar

This popular rooftop nightspot is famous for its open-air terrace that overlooks Millennium Park and Lake Michigan. Located in the architecturally stunning Chicago Athletic Association Hotel (▷ 112), advanced reservations are recommended. Steep prices, but worth it for the views, quality food and drink.

🔲 F10 ✉ 12 S. Michigan Avenue
☎ 312/792-3502 🚇 Brown, Green, Red, Pink, Purple Lines: Madison/Wabash 🚌 3, 4, 12

JAY PRITZKER PAVILION

grantparkmusicfestival.com

From June to August the Grant Park Music Festival holds free classical, jazz and pop concerts on Wednesday, Friday and Saturday evenings. The Grant Park Orchestra and visiting guests play.

🔲 G9 ✉ 201 E. Randolph Drive
☎ 312/742-1168 🚇 Brown, Green, Orange Lines: Randolph 🚌 127, 144, 146, 151

JOAN W. AND IRVING B. HARRIS THEATER FOR MUSIC AND DANCE

harristheaterchicago.org

Popular Harris theater hosts a 1,500-seat venue devoted primarily to performances of both local and visiting dance troupes.

GRANT PARK'S BLUES AND JAZZ

Each June and September the Petrillo Music Shell in Grant Park (▷ 51) is the stage for blues and jazz festivals respectively, which draw top international names as well as the city's greats in both fields. The performers are greeted by tens of thousands of fans, who arrive with blankets and picnic supplies to enjoy the free music.

🔲 G9 ✉ 205 E. Randolph Drive
☎ 312/334-7777 🚇 Brown, Green, Orange Lines: Randolph 🚌 127, 144, 146, 151

LOLLAPALOOZA

lollapalooza.com

One of the most popular music festivals in the US, this four-day summer festival draws dozens of big-name A-list and buzzed about rock, alternative, hip-hop and punk bands. Dance, comedy and crafts are a popular part of the festival, as is Kidzapalooza, an area which holds kids' rock concerts and different music activities. Buy tickets for Lollapalooza when they go on sale in spring, because they sell out fast.

🔲 G12 ✉ Grant Park (▷ 51) 🚇 Brown, Orange Lines: Randolph, Madison or Adams
☎ 888/512-7469 (tickets) 🚌 3, 4, 6, 38, 60, 145, 146, 147, 151, 157

Where to Eat

COLUMBUS TAP ($$)

columbustap.com

In the Fairmont Hotel, this bright, modern gastropub specializes in Midwestern food and serves locally brewed beers.

F9 200 N. Columbus Drive
312/444-9494 Lunch, dinner daily; open til midnight Brown, Green, Red, Pink, Purple Lines: Randolph/Wabash 146

MCKINLOCK COURT RESTAURANT ($$–$$$)

artic.edu/mckinlock-court-dining

Offering alfresco dining in the museum's courtyard spring through fall, the airy restaurant serves contemporary cuisine.

F10 111 S. Michigan Avenue
312/553-9675 Lunch daily and Thu 5–7.30pm Brown, Green, Orange Lines: Adams 127, 144, 146, 151

THE PALM ($$$$)

thepalm.com

One of the upscale Palm steak house chain serving massive steaks and chops, catering to the who's who enshrined in caricatures on the restaurant walls.

G9 323 E. Wacker Drive 312/616-1000 Lunch and dinner daily Brown, Green, Orange Lines: Randolph 143, 144, 145, 146, 151

PARK GRILL ($$$)

parkgrillchicago.com

Millennium Park's signature restaurant overlooks the skating rink in winter and uses the pavilion for outdoor dining in summer. Lunch options focus on hamburgers, pastas and salads. Dinner features American classics.

F10 11 N. Michigan Avenue
312/521-7275 Lunch and dinner daily Brown, Green, Orange Lines: Randolph 127, 144, 146, 151

SOUNDINGS CAFÉ ($$)

sheddaquarium.org

Panoramic lake views wrap the family-friendly casual café and coffee shop at the Shedd Aquarium. The menu features organic, locally grown produce for dishes like salads and sandwiches.

G12 1200 S. Lake Shore Drive
312/692-3277 Breakfast and lunch daily Green, Orange, Red Lines: Roosevelt 12, 127

TAVERN AT THE PARK ($$$)

tavernatthepark.com

The Tavern is a sophisticated place offering traditional American food with a contemporary twist, and it often features in lists of top Chicago restaurants. Try their signature Cloud Gate Martini, and one of the meat dishes for which they're renowned.

F9 130 E. Randolph Street Lunch and dinner. Closed Sun 312/552-0070 Brown, Orange Lines: Madison 3, 4, 60, 145, 147, 151

THE TASTE OF CHICAGO

Chicagoans love to eat and do so with gusto by the thousand at the annual Taste of Chicago festival in Grant Park. Usually held in July, around 100 local restaurants dispense their creations, often in affordable "taste-size" portions, from open-front stalls. Free entertainment keeps toes tapping.

Chicago's most chic shopping district, the Magnificent Mile, and priciest residential districts, including the Gold Coast, abut one another north of the Chicago River. Parks buffer the lakeshore.

Sights	58–72
Walk	73
Shopping	74–75
Entertainment and Nightlife	76–78
Where to Eat	78–80

Top 25   TOP 25

360 Chicago ▷ 58
Gallery Hopping ▷ 60
Lincoln Park Zoo ▷ 62
Navy Pier ▷ 64
North Avenue Beach ▷ 66
Second City ▷ 67
Shopping the Magnificent
  Mile ▷ 68

Lake

Michigan

Oak Street
Beach

East Lake Shore Drive

360
CHICAGO
East Delaware Place

Chestnut Street

Pearson Street
Seneca
Park
AVENUE
**Museum of
Contemporary Art**

Superior Street

Huron Street

St Clair Street
Erie Street

ONTARIO

**Weber May
Museum of Art** STREET
Museum of
Contemporary
Art

Illinois St

NBC
Tower

North Water Street
**Centennial Fountain
& Arc**

Chicago

LAKE STREET

NORTH

FAIRBANKS COURT

McCLURG COURT

East Grand Avenue

East Illinois Street

NORTH SHORE DRIVE

Outer
Harbor

Milton Lee
Olive Park

Ohio Street
Beach

**Chicago
Children's
Museum**

Navy Pier

NORTH STREETER DRIVE

DuSable
Park Site

G   H   J

360 Chicago

● 80-mile (129km) visibility
● Views of the skyline at night
● Lean out over the top of the building in a clear-glass box, on the thrill-seeking experience TILT.

Ride the elevator to 360 Chicago on the 94th floor of the city's iconic skyscraper, the John Hancock Center, for expansive views—by day or by night.

The observatory There are far-reaching vistas in every direction at 360 Chicago where, on a clear day, visitors can see for 80 miles (129km) and four surrounding states. An entertaining multimedia tour, included in the admission price, highlights the skyscrapers and Chicago history. For an extra fee, thrill-seekers can try the innovative TILT, which literally tilts people over the edge of the skyscraper in a glass box, so they face down to the street 1,000 feet (305m) below. A second admission after dark allows you to admire the city's skyline in all its twinkling glory.

Clockwise from left: visitors enjoy far-reaching views; the spectacular city view and beyond, looking down from 360 Chicago; the TILT is not for the fainthearted

The building Solid at its base and tapering as it goes skyward, the John Hancock Center, designed by the renowned firm Skidmore, Owings & Merrill, is divided nearly equally between residential and commercial use and, at 1,500 feet (457.2m), is the fourth-highest building in Chicago. It was constructed using a revolutionary external strengthening system, getting away from traditional internal pillars and thus creating more usable space on each floor. For more views go to the Signature Room restaurant (no admission charge) on the 95th floor. With unreserved seating, patrons have to dash for the best windowside seats when they become available, though all the tables have good sightlines. Sunsets draw a crowd, but it's really after sundown when the lights come up that the lounge is at its most romantic.

THE BASICS

360chicago.com

F7

⊠ John Hancock Center, 875 N. Michigan Avenue

☎ 360 Chicago: 888/875-8439; John Hancock Center: 312/751-3680

🕐 Daily 9am–11pm

🍴 Architect's Café and Bar (at 360 Chicago); Signature Room At The 95th

🚇 Red Line: Chicago

🚌 143, 144, 145, 146, 151

♿ Some

💰 360 Chicago: Expensive

Gallery Hopping in River North

HIGHLIGHTS

● Roy Boyd Gallery
● Carl Hammer Gallery
● Weinberg/Newton Gallery
● Byron Roche Gallery
● Zolla/Lieberman Gallery
● Maya Polsky Gallery

Dozens of art dealers occupy the former warehouses in River North's most handsome district for one-stop art shopping. Tours of galleries happen on Saturday.

From industry to art Chicago's gallery district claims roughly 70 art sellers in the heart of River North bounded by Chicago Avenue on the north, the Chicago River on the south, LaSalle to the east and Orleans to the west. The area boomed with industry, beginning in the 1890s when railroad tracks lined the north bank of the Chicago River, earning it the nickname "Smokey Hollow." River North slid slowly into decay as factories gradually closed in the 1950s and '60s. In the 1970s, attracted by low rents and large spaces, artists began to move in. Later, galleries followed, cementing the art

The Roy Boyd Gallery

NORTH SIDE TOP 25

scene in the district of redbrick warehouse buildings. Chain restaurants and condos have more recently driven up rents, but the galleries clustered on Huron and Superior streets have managed to survive the real-estate rush. The River North Design District contains showrooms filled with one-of-a-kind home decor items.

Art scene The most established artists showing in Chicago exhibit here alongside national and international names. Maya Polsky Gallery shows works by the late Ed Paschke, Roy Boyd Gallery exhibits the oils of Dan Devening and Carl Hammer Gallery displays Mr. Imagination, whose medium is bottle caps. All are open to the public but to visit with a guide, be at Starbuck's at 750 N. Franklin Street at 11am any Saturday, where the free tours kick off.

🞢 D7
✉ Between the Chicago River and Chicago Avenue, LaSalle and Orleans streets
🕐 Gallery hours vary; most open Tue–Sat 10–6
🍴 Restaurants, cafés and coffee shops nearby
🚊 Brown Line: Chicago
🚌 66
♿ Good
⚑ Free

Lincoln Park Zoo

HIGHLIGHTS

● Regenstein African
Journey
● Regenstein Center for
African Apes
● Kovler Seal Pool
● Walter Family Arctic
Tundra
● Penguin Cove
● Endangered Species
Carousel
● Pritzker Family Children's
Zoo

TIP

● Arrive at the sea lion
pool in time to see the daily
2pm feeding.

**Free to the public and a city block from
a popular residential district, the zoo is a
local favorite showcasing wild animals as
well as a dairy farm.**

Small beginnings Created out of sand dunes,
swamp and the former city cemetery, Lincoln
Park was established by the 1870s after its zoo
had been started with the gift of two swans
from New York's Central Park. Evolving over
several years through the contributions of
various designers, it is one of the oldest zoos
in the country.

Wild kingdom The zoo, a block east of a smart
residential district, is very much a part of city life
where passersby can drop in on the lion pride
or the swimming polar bears. Early 20th-century

Clockwise from left: A polar bear cooling off; giraffe; Lincoln Park Zoo entrance; tigers grooming each other; the zoo is colorfully lit up at night; the gorilla enclosure

brick buildings house the big cats, mammals and some monkeys, but a spate of new building has brought more immersive exhibits to the zoo. The Regenstein African Journey creates an atmospheric passage through habitats for pygmy hippos, deerlike klipspringers, wild dogs, towering giraffes and even cockroaches. The Regenstein Center for African Apes lets the light shine into vine-covered and bamboo-planted indoor living areas, supplemented by outdoor grounds. The Children's Zoo combines a climbing area and interactive exhibits.

Down on the farm Farm-in-the-Zoo's white-trimmed red barn is one of Chicago's more unusual buildings. The farmyard teaches kids where food comes from with presentations on milking, butter-churning and egg hatching.

THE BASICS

lpzoo.org

🔢 E3

✉ 2001 N. Clark Street

☎ 312/742-2000

🕐 Apr–May, Sep–Oct daily 10–5; Nov–Mar 10–4.30

🚇 Brown, Purple Lines: Armitage

🚌 22, 36, 151, 156

♿ Good

💷 Free

Navy Pier

TOP 25

HIGHLIGHTS

- Ferris wheel
- Chicago Children's Museum
- Chicago Shakespeare Theater
- Boat rides
- AMC Navy Pier IMAX® Theatre
- Views of city from the pier
- Family Pavilion Stage

TIP

- The popular beer garden at the end of the pier serves draft beer, snacks and a line-up of local bands in summer, with great skyline views.

One of the region's most popular destinations, Navy Pier is an evolving mix of culture, cuisine, entertainment and retail. A redesigned entrance plaza with a fountain greets visitors, who can stroll the pier snapping photos of the gorgeous skyline and Lake Michigan.

History and cruises Opened in 1916, Navy Pier was part of architect Daniel Burnham's vision for a new Chicago and combined shipping with dining and entertainment. The former steadily disappeared and the pier declined until a 1990s makeover saw it re-emerge as a stylish family-aimed entertainment venue in the heart of the city. The pier has encouraged a revival of water activity with a plethora of pleasure cruises departing from its edge along Dock Street.

Clockwise from left: Navy Pier Ferris Wheel; fountain outside the Children's Museum; the city provides a dramatic backdrop to Navy Pier

Entertainment Enclosed gondolas make it possible to ride the new, 196-foot (60-m) high Centennial Ferris Wheel year-round. Crowds also come for the boat rides, children's museum, IMAX movies, a dancing water fountain for children to splash around in, motorized swings that spin 14ft (4m) off the floor, and more. On summer nights, sit in the beer garden and listen to live music while watching the fireworks shows.

Culture Take in a concert at one of Navy Pier's several stages. For intellectual balance, get tickets to the acclaimed Chicago Shakespeare Theater, modeled on the venues of the Bard's own day with seating surrounding the stage on three levels. The Chicago Children's Museum educates as it entertains (▷ 69).

THE BASICS

navypier.com

➕ H8

✉ 600 E. Grand Avenue

☎ 312/595-7437

🕐 Jun–Sep Fri–Sat 10am–midnight, Sun–Thu 10–10; Apr–May Fri–Sat 10–10, Sun–Thu 10–8; Jan–Mar Fri–Sat 10–10, Mon–Thu 10–8, Sun 10–7

🍴 Various restaurants and cafés

🚆 Red Line: Grand

🚌 29, 56, 65, 66

♿ Good

🎫 Free; fee for individual attractions

North Avenue Beach

TOP 25

Outdoor activities at North Avenue Beach

HIGHLIGHTS

- Beach volleyball
- Chess Pavilion
- Ocean-liner bathhouse
- Upper-deck Castaways Bar & Grill
- Seasonal outdoor gym
- Swimming

Daily in summer, and especially on weekends and holidays, Chicagoans storm this beach, one of the liveliest and best equipped of the city's 33 strands on the 31-mile (50km) Lake Michigan shore.

Games for all To mingle with Chicagoans, head to North Avenue Beach, a community playground for families, young singles, exercise fanatics and people watchers. The park is known as a volleyballer's delight, lined with net uprights (players provide the nets and balls) used by teams as well as casual pick-up players. A temporary stadium showcases professional players when they come to town in July. Or you can head to the Chess Pavilion on the concrete biking and walking path south of the beach. Yoga classes are held both on the sand, and balancing on paddleboards in the lake. While you can watch Chicago's annual August Air and Water Show from beaches up and down the shore, the main action takes place at North Avenue, drawing many of the million people a day who view the displays.

Bathhouse The ocean-liner-looking building beached on the shore replaced the original landmark Depression-era bathhouse of the same design. The 2000 version has showers, restrooms and concession stands as well as beach chair, bike and volleyball equipment rentals. Singles go to Castaways Bar & Grill for margaritas and beer, though it also serves salads and sandwiches.

Detail of the building's exterior (left); outside the theater (middle and right)

Second City

From the stage at Second City, Chicago performers, including some very famous cast members, popularized a form of improvised comedy now enjoyed on television and in cities around the world.

Their laurels Chicago's signature brand of bold, broad and quick wit was nurtured and became popular at Second City. Since 1959 the Old Town comedy theater has been training actors such as *Saturday Night Live* cast members John Belushi, Bill Murray and Gilda Radner. Other alumni who have passed through the theater and on to lucrative film gigs include Dan Ackroyd, Mike Myers of *Austin Powers* fame and actor Steve Carell. Shows bear names like "Truth, Justice or the American Way," riffing on current events, pop culture and the American political scene.

Improv comedy Improvisational comedy relies on the actors supplying the dialog and the direction. They call for audience suggestions and incorporate those into the action in a form known as "spot improv," popular at Second City. Theater historians trace improv back to early Europe's Commedia dell 'Arte in which theater troupes traveled from town to town performing in public squares and improvising the script based on a theme. With thought to making theater more generally accessible, a group of actors founded The Compass in 1950s' Chicago, which later became Second City and went on to influence performers worldwide.

THE BASICS

secondcity.com
➕ E4
✉ 161 N. Wells Street
☎ 312/337-3992
🕐 Tue–Thu 8, Fri–Sat 8 and 11, Sun 7
Ⓜ Red Line: Clark Street
🚌 72, 156
♿ Fair
💵 Expensive

HIGHLIGHTS

● Improv shows on two separate stages
● Cabaret seating
● Central Old Town location near restaurants and bars
● Up Comedy Club

NORTH SIDE TOP 25

67

Shopping the Magnificent Mile

Wrigley Building on Magnificent Mile; Tiffany's (centre); shoppers throng the sidewalk (right)

THE BASICS

themagnificentmile.com

➕ F8

✉ Michigan Avenue north of the Chicago River to its terminus at Oak Street

☎ 312/409-5560 (events)

🚇 Red Line: Chicago, Grand

🚌 143, 144, 145, 146, 151

♿ Good

HIGHLIGHTS

● Water Tower and Pumping Station
● Bloomingdale's
● Nordstrom
● Saks Fifth Avenue
● Crate & Barrel
● Ralph Lauren

From the Chicago River to Oak Street Beach, this portion of Michigan Avenue known as Chicago's Magnificent Mile lines up designer boutiques and major department stores in one bustling stretch.

Shop till you drop Over 460 stores pack the mile, selling something for everyone from designer goods by Salvatore Ferragamo, precious jewelry at Cartier and the tailored suits of Brooks Brothers to off-price fashions from Swedish retailer H&M. Between high and low ends are the major American department stores, including Nordstrom, known for its clothes and shoe selection; Neiman Marcus, famed for its clientele and designer racks; and Bloomingdale's, with its on-trend looks. Vertical malls such as 900 North Michigan house Bloomingdale's, and Water Tower Place, home to Macy's, houses shops such as cook's favorite Williams-Sonoma and Coach leatherware. Mothers and daughters flock to American Girl Place, a doll store with accessories.

Culture breaks Architectural icons line the street, making this a good walk even for the shop shy. The Wrigley Building and the Chicago Tribune Building face each other on the south end of the street. Farther north, the historic Water Tower and Pumping Station, two of the few to survive the Great Fire of 1871, symbolize the city's rebirth on the thoroughfare. A block from Michigan Avenue, the Museum of Contemporary Art shows cutting-edge work.

More to See

CHICAGO CHILDREN'S MUSEUM

chicagochildrensmuseum.org
There are three floors of scores of entertaining things to do for those under 12 including workshop areas such as the Tinkering Lab, where children use real tools and materials to create things, the Dinosaur Expedition and Treehouse Trails. In the Story Hub, a fabulous multimedia area, children can make short movies (which they can then access online) about their visit to their favorite areas of the museum. The programs change daily.

H8 ⊠ Navy Pier, 700 E. Grand Avenue ☎ 312/527-1000 🕐 Daily 10–5 (till 8 on Thu) Ⓡ Red Line: Grand 🚌 29, 56, 65, 66 ♿ Good 💲 Moderate; free Thu 5–8

CHICAGO HISTORY MUSEUM

chicagohistory.org
Spread throughout a Georgian-style brick building constructed in 1932, with a modern, glass-walled extension, every major facet in Chicago's rise from swampland to modern metropolis is discussed and beautifully illustrated in chronologically arranged galleries. Alongside changing temporary shows, there are outstanding permanent exhibits including Chicago: Crossroads of America and Lincoln's Chicago. The Museum also has an extensive costume and textile collection including articles from world-renowned fashion designers as well as household textiles by artists such as Angelo Testa.

E4 ⊠ 1601 N. Clark Street ☎ 312/642-4600 🕐 Mon–Sat 9.30–4.30, Sun 12–5 Ⓡ Brown Line: Sedgwick 🚌 11, 22, 36, 72, 151, 156 ♿ Good 💲 Moderate; free Mon

FOURTH PRESBYTERIAN CHURCH

fourthchurch.org
This Gothic Revival church (1914) serves a congregation of Chicago's elite. It was the creation of American architect Ralph Adams Cram. Occasional but enjoyable lunchtime concerts pack the pews.

F7 ⊠ 126 E. Chestnut Street

NORTH SIDE MORE TO SEE

Chicago Children's Museum

69

☎ 312/787-4570 ⏰ Mon–Fri 7.30am–9pm, Sat 7.30–6, Sun 7.30–6.30 🚇 Red Line: Chicago 🚌 145, 146, 147, 151 ♿ Good

THE GOLD COAST
In the late 19th century, Chicago businessman Potter Palmer astonished his peers by erecting a mansion home on undeveloped land well north of the Loop close to Lake Michigan. As others followed, the area became known as the Gold Coast, its streets lined by the elegant homes of the well-to-do.
✚ F5

HISTORIC WATER TOWER
This pseudo-Gothic confection, built by William Boyington in 1869 in yellow limestone, is one of Chicago's enduring landmarks and is the oldest building on the north side of the Chicago river.
✚ F7 ✉ 806 N. Michigan Avenue ☎ First-floor photography gallery: 312/742-0808 ⏰ Daily 10–6.30 (holidays 10–4) 🚇 Red Line: Chicago 🚌 3, 145, 146, 147, 151 ♿ Few 🎫 Free

HOLY NAME CATHEDRAL
holynamecathedral.org
This is the seat of the Catholic Archdiocese of Chicago (1878). Built after the Great Chicago Fire of 1871, its cornerstone was laid in 1874. The cathedral features a towering Gothic Revival design.
✚ F7 ✉ 735 N. State Street ☎ 312/787-8040 🚇 Red Line: Chicago 🚌 29, 36 ♿ Good ❓ Check website for tours

INTERNATIONAL MUSEUM OF SURGICAL SCIENCES
imss.org
The museum's floors, as well as temporary shows, cover health and medicine-related subjects. Among the oldest exhibits are drilled skulls from Peruvian temples, and surgeon's tools found at Pompeii. Many rooms have displays of needles and other metallic things.
✚ F5 ✉ 1524 N. Lake Shore Drive ☎ 312/642-6502 ⏰ Tue–Fri 10–4, Sat–Sun 10–5 🚇 Brown Line: Sedgwick 🚌 151 ♿ Good 💰 Moderate; free on Tue ❓ Guided tour Sat 2pm

The Hall of Mortals at the International Museum of Surgical Sciences

Historic Water Tower

LINCOLN PARK CONSERVATORY

lincolnparkconservancy.org

The Conservatory (1891) has four separate greenhouses: The Orchid House, Fern Room, Show House and Palm House. Each one contains dazzling tropical and subtropical blooms as well as seasonal displays. Beyond the greenhouses there are magnificent gardens in different styles, a fountain and a Shakespeare monument.

➕ E2 ✉ 2391 N. Stockton Drive
☎ Conservatory: 312/742-7736 🕐 Daily 9–5 Ⓡ Red Line: Armitage 🚌 76, 77, 145, 146, 147, 151, 156 ♿ Good 💲 Free

MUSEUM OF CONTEMPORARY ART

mcachicago.org

Highlights from the permanent collection include the works of Chicago-based Ed Paschke, and Richard Long's *Chicago Mud Circle* (1996), created directly on a gallery wall. The lower levels house temporary exhibitions and provide access to the Sculpture Garden. A guide can take you on a free tour of the exhibitions and collection. Cutting-edge dance, theater, and music performances take place at the Edlis Neeson Theater.

➕ F7 ✉ 220 E. Chicago Avenue
☎ 312/280-2660 🕐 Tue 10–8, Wed–Sun 10–5 🍴 Café Ⓡ Red Line: Chicago 🚌 157 ♿ Good 💲 Moderate; free on Tue
❓ Guided tours daily (45 min)

OAK STREET BEACH

The closeness of the exclusive Gold Coast neighborhood helps make Oak Street Beach the gathering place for some of Chicago's richest and best-toned bodies. See the huge mural at the Oak Street Beach underpass access.

➕ F6 ✉ Access from junction of N. Michigan Avenue and E. Lake Shore Drive
🚌 145, 146, 147, 151

OLD TOWN

oldtownchicago.org

Gentrified in the 1960s and '70s by artists, the Old Town area combines

Beautiful floral displays surround the Conservatory in Lincoln Park

busy, restaurant-lined commercial throughways and intimate leafy residential streets. The annual June art fair is a big draw.

✚ D5 ✉ Streets fan out from intersection of North Avenue and Wells Street 🚇 Brown Line: Sedgwick 🚌 11, 72, 156

THE PEGGY NOTEBAERT NATURE MUSEUM

naturemuseum.org

Lively exhibits explore the natural history of the Midwest, including a greenhouse holding Butterfly Haven, and the inside story on the insect population of every household.

✚ E2 ✉ On banks of North Pond in Lincoln Park ☎ 773/755-5100 🕐 Mon–Fri 9–5, Sat–Sun 10–5 🚇 Brown, Red Lines: Fullerton 🚌 22, 36, 72, 156 ♿ Good 💲 Moderate; donations

THE TRIBUNE TOWER

In the 1920s, the *Chicago Tribune* staged a competition to decide the design of its new premises. The resulting neo-Gothic building is best admired from the exterior, inlaid with 120 stones from sites around the world including Greece's Parthenon and India's Taj Mahal. A change of ownership in the fall of 2016 brings with it a mixed-use development plan.

✚ F8 ✉ 435 N. Michigan Avenue ☎ 312/222-9100 🚇 Red Line: Grand 🚌 3, 11, 29, 65, 147, 151, 157 ♿ Good

THE WRIGLEY BUILDING

Partly modeled on the Giralda Tower in Seville, Spain, although the ornamental features echo the French Renaissance, the North and South structures stand behind a facade linked by an arcaded walkway at street level and by two enclosed aerial walkways. The ornate glazed terra-cotta facade has retained its original gleam. Come back at night to see the building beautifully illuminated.

✚ F8 ✉ 400 N. Michigan Avenue ☎ 312/923-8080 🕐 Business hours 🚇 Red Line: Grand 🚌 3, 11, 29, 65, 147, 151, 157 ♿ Good 💲 Free

The Wrigley Building

The ornate entrance to the Tribune Tower

One Magnificent Walk

Take in several architectural icons as well as the glitziest shopping in a mile-long walk up Michigan Avenue from the Chicago River.

DISTANCE: 1 mile (1.6 km) **ALLOW:** 2–3 hours

START · END

MICHIGAN AVENUE BRIDGE 🚇 Red
Line: Grand 🚌 3, 11, 29, 65, 147, 151, 157

JOHN HANCOCK CENTER (▷ 58)
🚇 Red Line: Chicago 🚌 145, 146, 147, 151

❶ Leave the Loop by walking north across the Chicago River on Michigan Avenue Bridge, which in 1920 facilitated the rise of the so-called Magnificent Mile.

❷ Two of the first structures erected after the bridge was built were the Wrigley Building (1921–24), to the left, and the Tribune Tower (1925), to the right.

❸ Farther north, opulent shops and hotels line Michigan Avenue. Fuel some heavy-duty window shopping with a bag of cheese popcorn from Garrett Popcorn, 625 N. Michigan at the corner with Ontario.

❹ One of the liveliest stores is Nike Town between Erie and Huron streets. Farther north is the Disney Store.

❺ Cross to the west side of Michigan Avenue and continue to the junction with Chicago Avenue.

❻ Stop at the Historic Water Tower, which survived the Great Fire and now holds a photographic gallery. A good visitor information center is located in the old Pumping Station, opposite.

❼ A block north, at Chestnut Street, is the imposing Gothic form of the Fourth Presbyterian Church, used for lunch-time recitals. Cross back over Michigan Avenue to Water Tower Place, a glitzy, high-profile shopping mall.

❽ Finish the walk at the John Hancock Center (1970), where 360 Chicago affords stunning views.

Shopping

900 NORTH MICHIGAN

shop900.com

This gleaming marble high-rise takes up a whole city block. Restaurants, cinemas and many stores are grouped around a six-floor atrium; a branch of Bloomingdale's is an anchor. The vast building is also home to a number of smaller, exclusive stores.

➕ F7 ✉ 900 N. Michigan Avenue
☎ 312/915-3916 🚇 Red Line: Chicago
🚌 145, 146, 147, 151

AMERICAN GIRL PLACE

americangirl.com

At this doll store in Water Tower Place, you can not only buy a doll that looks like you but also get her hair styled, take her to tea and have your photo taken for the cover of a souvenir magazine.

➕ F7 ✉ 835 N. Michigan Avenue
☎ 877/247-5223 🚇 Red Line: Chicago
🚌 33, 143, 144, 145, 146, 147, 148, 151, X3

ATLAS GALLERIES

atlasgalleries.com

This leading gallery handles artwork from the Renaissance to Impressionists and contemporary works. A visit is as good as a trip to the museum.

RANDOLPH STREET MARKET

Hundreds of vendors pack the old union plumber's hall at 1350 W. Randolph Street one weekend each month to sell a treasure trove of fun and funky items, like vintage brooches, retro decor and gourmet desserts. Local artists and entrepreneurs also launch new products here. Live entertainment and local craft beers add to the liveliness. An admission fee is charged at the gate, but pay in advance online (randolphstreetmarket.com) and you'll save a few bucks.

➕ F8 ✉ 535 N. Michigan Avenue
☎ 312/329-9330 🚇 Red Line: Chicago
🚌 145, 146, 147, 151

BANANA REPUBLIC

bananarepublic.com

Popular local branch of the supplier of quality casualwear. Other stores at 835 N. Michigan and 900 N. Michigan.

➕ F8 ✉ 744 N. Michigan Avenue
☎ 312/642-0020 🚇 Red Line: Chicago
🚌 145, 146, 147, 151

BOURDAGE PEARLS

bourdagepearls.com

Journey to this northside jewelry gallery near Wrigley Field for its high-quality freshwater pearls.

➕ Off map C1 ✉ 4039A N. Ravenswood Avenue ☎ 773/244-1126 🚇 Brown Line: Irving Park 🚌 152

BROOKS BROTHERS

brooksbrothers.com

Well-made menswear, in conservative styles, plus some equally straightforward clothing for women.

➕ F8 ✉ 713 N. Michigan Avenue
☎ 312/915-0060 🚇 Red Line: Chicago
🚌 145, 146, 147, 151

ELEMENTS

elementschicago.com

From home decor to handbags, jewelry and fashion accessories, this treasure house of style and design features beautiful objects from around the world.

➕ E7 ✉ 741 N. Wells Street ☎ 877/642-6574
🚇 Brown, Purple Lines: Chicago 🚌 66, 156

J. CREW

jcrew.com

Classic modern clothes, shoes and accessories for young men and women to wear at work and for leisure.

📍 F7 ✉ 900 N. Michigan Avenue
☎ 312/751-2739 🚇 Red Line: Chicago
🚌 145, 146, 147, 151

KOKOROKOKO

kokorokokovintage.com
Miss the 1980s and '90s? This funky
Wicker Park vintage shop sells everything from cartoon buttons and stickers
to vintage overalls and T-shirts. Nothing
costs more than $100.
📍 A6 ✉ 822 N. Milwaukee Avenue
☎ 773/252-6996 🚇 Blue Line: Division
🚌 145, 146, 147, 151

NAVY PIER

navypier.com
Around 40 shops are gathered in this
complex of restaurants and entertainment venues. This is a good place if
you want souvenirs as gifts.
📍 H8 ✉ 600 E. Grand Avenue ☎ 312/595-
7437 🚇 Red Line: Grand 🚌 29, 56, 65, 66

NEIMAN-MARCUS

neimanmarcus.com
Elegant clothing is the forte of this store,
which also sells beauty products and
fancy food stuffs. Just browsing through
this store is fun.
📍 F8 ✉ 737 N. Michigan Avenue
☎ 312/642-5900 🚇 Red Line: Chicago
🚌 145, 146, 147, 151

P.O.S.H.

poshchicago.com
The expression "port out/starboard
home," used by aristocrats seeking the
shady side of the ship journeying
between Britain and India, lends its
name to this antiques shop specializing
in vintage tabletop items from the early
19th century.
📍 F8 ✉ 613 N. State Street ☎ 312/280-
1602 🚇 Red Line: Grand 🚌 22, 65

MAGNIFICENT MILE

Michigan Avenue, home to many top-class
and designer stores, is known as the
"Magnificent Mile," a 1940s concept that
eventually mutated into today's rows of
marble-clad towers, mostly built during
the 1970s and 1980s.

SAKS FIFTH AVENUE

saksfifthavenue.com
Saks is one of America's classiest
department stores, carrying name
designer labels and high-end decor
and household items.
📍 F8 ✉ 700 N. Michigan Avenue ☎ 312/
944-6500 🚇 Red Line: Chicago, Grand
🚌 145, 146, 147, 151

SHOPS AT THE MART

themart.com
Most of the vast Merchandise Mart is
closed to the public, except for the
first two floors, which woo shoppers
with clothing stores, gift shops and
food court.
📍 E9 ✉ 350 N. Wells Street ☎ 800/677-
6278 🚇 Brown, Purple Lines: Merchandise
Mart 🚌 11, 22, 37, 125, 134, 135, 136, 156

WATER TOWER PLACE

shopwatertower.com
Packing an incredible seven floors are
a diverse range of clothing stores for
men, women and children that span
Abercrombie & Fitch, Betsey Johnson,
French Connection and Victoria's Secret.
There is also a choice of jewelers, art
galleries, home-furnishing emporiums,
cinemas and restaurants, and specialty
retailers such as Accent Chicago and the
Water Tower Clock Shop.
📍 F7 ✉ 835 N. Michigan Avenue
☎ 312/440-3166 🚇 Red Line: Chicago
🚌 145, 146, 147, 151

Entertainment and Nightlife

ANDY'S JAZZ CLUB
andysjazzclub.com
This popular club has some of the best live jazz in the city, since the 1970s. Doors open about 4pm and dinner at 6pm; 4pm Friday & Saturday. Table reservations for dining only.
➕ F8 ✉ 11 E. Hubbard Street ☎ 312/642-6805 Ⓜ Red Line: Grand 🚌 29, 36

THE BATON SHOW LOUNGE
thebatonshowlounge.com
Female impersonators dressed like celebrities, sing and interact with the crowd at this rowdy, legendary drag show. The humor is bawdy, the costumes are elaborate, and the singers are talented and entertaining. Since it's a popular spot for bachelorette parties, reservations are recommended.
➕ E8 ✉ 436 N. Clark ☎ 312/ 644-5269 Ⓜ Red Line: Grand 🚌 22

THE BEAUTY BAR
thebeautybar.com
Manicures are given and martinis are served in the front of the bar until mid-night. Meanwhile, in the back, the bar turns into a college-like dance party with retro tunes by Madonna or '90s hits. Trivia nights, karaoke and other nightly events add to the fun.
➕ A7 ✉ 1444 W. Chicago Avenue ☎ 312/ 226-8828 Ⓜ Blue Line: Chicago 🚌 52, 77

NIGHTCLUB NEWS
The most general source is the Friday edition of the *Chicago Tribune* and its Metromix website (metromix.com). Inside info on the latest clubs, as well as the night-life scene in general, can be found in the pages of the weekly *Chicago Reader* and on the websites for *New City* and *Time Out Chicago* magazines.

BILLY GOAT TAVERN
billygoattavern.com
This below-street-level, unpretentious watering hole and cheeseburger joint is a favorite among local journalists. It's noted as the inspiration for a famous television comedy sketch.
➕ F8 ✉ 430 N. Michigan Avenue (also at Navy Pier) ☎ 312/222-1525 Ⓜ Red Line: Grand 🚌 145, 146, 147, 151

BLUE CHICAGO
bluechicago.com
This comfortable, homey blues club, has been showcasing home-grown musical talent for more than 30 years.
➕ E7 ✉ 534 N. Clark Street ☎ 312/661-0100 and 312/642-6261 Ⓜ Red Line: Chicago 🚌 22, 36 ♿ Good

B.L.U.E.S.
chicagobluesbar.com
One of the best little blues clubs in Chicago and worth the trip out, but get there early as it's a tiny venue. On Sunday nights your admission here will also get you into Kingston Mines (▷ 77).
➕ C1 ✉ 2519 N. Halsted Street ☎ 773/528-1012 Ⓜ Red, Brown Lines: Fullerton 🚌 8

THE CASTLE
This complex has four different clubs, each with a different take on nightlife, in an 1890s sandstone castle. Try Palladium, Cabaret or the Dome Room and then slide into street-level Craft for a late-night snack.
➕ E8 ✉ 632 N. Dearborn Street ☎ 312/ 266-1944 Ⓜ Red Line: Grand 🚌 22

CHICAGO SHAKESPEARE THEATER
chicagoshakes.com
A 500-seat auditorium on Navy Pier makes a fine setting for the works of the

Bard. Abridged "Short Shakespeare" and family musicals in summer.

🔷 H8 ✉ 800 E. Grand Avenue ☎ 312/595-5600 🚇 Red Line: Grand 🚌 29, 56, 65, 66

HOUSE OF BLUES

hob.com

Blues and rock from around the world every night. The smaller Back Porch stage has blues nightly and is open at lunch for more of the same. A gospel choir stars at Sunday brunch.

🔷 E9 ✉ 329 N. Dearborn Street ☎ 312/923-2000 🚇 Red Line: Grand 🚌 22, 36, 62

JAZZ SHOWCASE

jazzshowcase.com

Photos of jazz legends decorate this historic joint, opened in 1947 by Joe Segal, and big names play here. Bring the kids to the Sunday matinee.

🔷 E8 ✉ Dearborn Station, 806 S. Plymouth Court ☎ 312/360-0234 🚇 Red Line: Grand 🚌 22, 65

KINGSTON MINES

kingstonmines.com

Regularly voted Chicago's best blues club, this place has been in business since 1968. Known for their barbecue, this is a place for ribs, Louisiana catfish, Cajun chicken, jambalaya and a host of other specialties. It's way off the track for most visitors, so only those in the know head out here.

🔷 C1 ✉ 2548 N. Halsted Street ☎ 773/477-4646 🚇 Red, Brown Lines: Fullerton 🚌 8

LOOKINGGLASS THEATRE

lookingglasstheatre.org

Housed in the Water Tower Pumping Station, the troupe is lauded for its experimental staging and use of exciting circus arts.

🔷 F7 ✉ 821 N. Michigan Avenue ☎ 312/337-0665 🚇 Red Line: Chicago 🚌 66, 143, 144, 145, 146, 151

PARK WEST

parkwestchicago.com

Intimate size and strong acoustics make this the ideal place for music, be it folk, jazz, rock or something else from the eclectic program.

🔷 D3 ✉ 322 W. Armitage Avenue ☎ 773/929-1322 🚇 Brown, Red Lines: Armitage 🚌 23, 72

ROSA'S LOUNGE

rosaslounge.com

Less touristy than other Chicago blues clubs, the friendly owners welcome you to watch intimate shows by talented blues musicians.

🔷 D3 ✉ 322 W. Armitage Avenue ☎ 773/342-0452 🚇 Blue Line: Damen 🚌 73

SECOND CITY

secondcity.com

Biting satire and inspired improvisation have made this a legendary comedy club that's launched the careers of many stars. They're so successful that a second Second City stage offers a separate cast and show (▷ 67). The adjacent Up Comedy Club features stand-up comedians.

🔷 E5 ✉ 1616 N. Wells Street ☎ 773/337-3992 🚇 Brown Line: Sedgwick 🚌 11, 156

NORTH SIDE ENTERTAINMENT AND NIGHTLIFE

SPY BAR

spybarchicago.com

Go underground to this clubbing institution, where the decks have been spinning for the past 18 years and the party pulses amid exposed brick walls and velvet couches. The entrance is through an alleyway.

🞦 E7 ✉ 646 N. Franklin Street ☎ 312/337-2191 🚇 Brown Line: Chicago 🚌 37

STEPPENWOLF THEATRE

steppenwolf.org

Home of the enormously successful Steppenwolf repertory company, founded in 1976, and still a premier

venue for the best of Off-Loop theater. The theater has a 900-seat main hall and two smaller spaces for experimental drama. High-profile members include John Malkovich.

🞦 C4 ✉ 1650 N. Halsted Street ☎ 312/335-1650 🚇 Red Line: North/Clybourn 🚌 8, 72

ZANIES

chicago.zanies.com

Zanies has been making people laugh for nearly 40 years. This intimate comedy club, features rising local stars as well as better-known names.

🞦 E5 ✉ 1548 N. Wells Street ☎ 312/337-4027 🚇 Brown Line: Sedgwick 🚌 11, 156

Where to Eat

PRICES
Prices are approximate, based on a 3-course meal for one person.
$$$$ over $50
$$$ $31–$50
$$ $16–$30
$ up to $15

ADOBO GRILL ($$)

adobogrill.com

Authentic Mexican dishes in a convivial atmosphere just below Second City. Also, there are 100 tequilas on offer.

🞦 E5 ✉ 215 W. North Avenue ☎ 312/266-7999 🕓 Mon–Sat dinner, Sunday brunch 🚇 Red Line: Clark/Division 🚌 72, 156

ALINEA ($$$$)

alinea-restaurant.com

Chef Grant Achatz practices a form of alchemy at Alinea. He incorporates

science in deconstructing dishes that are presented on custom serving pieces such as aromatic pillows. For bold and liberal tastes only. Reservations must be made at least six weeks in advance.

🞦 C4 ✉ 1723 N. Halsted ☎ 312/867-0110 🕓 Wed–Sun dinner only. Closed Mon–Tue 🚇 Brown Line: Armitage 🚌 8

BIG BOWL CAFÉ ($–$$)

bigbowl.com

Delectable Chinese noodle dishes and Thai curries served in big bowls.

🞦 F6 ✉ 60 E. Ohio Street ☎ 312/951-1888 🕓 Daily lunch and dinner 🚇 Brown Line: Chicago 🚌 37, 41

BIN 36 ($–$$$)

bin36.com

Convivial River North loft-cum-wine-bar café pours dozens of selections by the glass and in wine "flights" or tasting

portions paired to French-influenced American food and a 50-offering cheese bar. Seating ranges from café tables to stools at the zinc-topped bar.

⊞ E9 ✉ 339 N. Dearborn Street
☎ 312/755-9463 🕐 Mon–Sat dinner. Closed Sun 🚇 Red Line: Grand 🚌 22

BISTRONOMIC ($$$)

bistronomic.net/hostalt

Comfortable, modern contemporary setting for eclectic dining with New American, Provincial French and modern European tones.

⊞ F7 ✉ 840 N. Wabash Avenue
☎ 312/944-8400 🕐 Dinner daily, Wed–Sun lunch 🚇 Red Line: Chicago 🚌 66

DOVE'S LUNCHEONETTE ($$)

Grab a seat at the counter of this adorable Wicker Park restaurant, where '60s and '70s Chicago soul and blues plays on the juke box. The menu's a mix of breakfast, American comfort food and contemporary Mexican.

✉ 1545 N. Damen Avenue ☎ 773/645-4060 🕐 Daily breakfast, lunch and dinner 🚇 Blue Line: Damen 🚌 50

FRONTERA GRILL/ TOPOLOBAMPO ($$$–$$$$)

fronterakitchens.com

Chef Rick Bayless introduced the nation to regional Mexican food from his Frontera Grill hot spot in River North. Next to it is Topolobampo, its fine dining counterpart.

⊞ E8 ✉ 445 N. Clark Street ☎ 312/661-1434 🕐 Closed Sun–Mon 🚇 Red Line: Grand 🚌 22

GENE & GEORGETTI ($$$$)

geneandgeorgetti.com

Many feel that this steak house, with its men's-club decor, gruff waiters and

deliciously thick cuts of meat, is the best in the city. Non-carnivores beware though, there's scant choice.

⊞ E8 ✉ 500 N. Franklin Street ☎ 312/527-3718 🕐 Closed Sun 🚇 Brown, Purple Lines: Merchandise Mart 🚌 37

GRAND LUX CAFÉ ($$–$$$)

grandluxcafe.com

With an opulent and spacious interior, the Lux serves up a truly international menu, from Jamaican jerk chicken to veal saltimbocca. Whether you want a tasty meal or just a break from shopping, the Lux is hard to beat.

⊞ F8 ✉ 600 N. Michigan Avenue
☎ 312/276-2500 🕐 Daily lunch and dinner, Sat–Sun brunch also 🚇 Red Line: Grand 🚌 143, 144, 145, 146, 151

IL PORCELLINO ($$$)

ilporcellinochicago.com

Great Italian-American classics are served in this classy restaurant, with club-like chairs, stone walls and mood lighting. Ingredients are locally sourced from artisan growers. The resident mixologist prepares good cocktails too.

⊞ E8 ✉ 59 W. Hubbard Street ☎ 312/595-0800 🕐 Daily dinner 🚇 Red Line: Grand 🚌 22

HOT DOGS

To a Chicagoan, a hot dog is not merely a frank in a bun. The true Chicago hot dog is a Viennese beef sausage smeared with mustard, relish, onions and hot peppers to taste. Brightly lit hot-dog outlets are a feature of the city. Among them are Gold Coast Dogs:

✉ 159 N. Wabash Avenue, and other locations ☎ 312/917-1677
🕐 Breakfast, lunch, dinner. Closed Sat–Sun 🚇 Red line: Grand 🚌 29, 36

MAGGIANO'S LITTLE ITALY ($$–$$$)

maggianos.com

One of the best and yet best-value Italians in town, which manages to be both smart yet informal, and always busy. Try the baked *ziti* (a type of pasta) and sausage or lobster ravioli.

⊕ E8 ✉ 516 N. Clark Street ☎ 312/644-7700 🕐 Daily lunch and dinner, Sat–Sun brunch also 🚇 Red Line: Grand 🚌 22, 65

MORTON'S OF CHICAGO ($$$)

mortons.com

This is a place for steak lovers. Chicago takes steak seriously, and here the Porterhouses are grilled to perfection. The service is excellent too.

⊕ E7 ✉ 1050 N. State Street ☎ 312/266-4820 🕐 Daily dinner 🚇 Red Line: Chicago 🚌 36

PUB ROYALE ($$$)

pubroyale.com

You'll find an outstanding beer selection that compliments perfectly the British-Indian menu in this wildly decorated Wicker Park hangout. A whole section is devoted to Royale Cups fruity cocktails, made with a version of Pimm's.

✉ 2049 W. Division ☎ 773/661-6874 🕐 Fri–Sun lunch and dinner, Mon–Thu dinner only 🚇 Blue Line: Damen 🚌 50, 70

PIZZA!

Chicago is where the deep-dish pizza was invented, but by who? One contender is Gino's East (locations include ✉ 162 E. Superior Street ☎ 312/266-3337), but Pizzeria Uno (✉ 29 E. Ohio Street ☎ 312/321-1000) also claims to have been first. Stuffed pizzas, with a crust top and bottom, are also a Chicago specialty. For this, try Giordano's (✉ 730 N. Rush Street ☎ 312/951-0747 and other locations).

RIVA ($$$)

rivanavypier.com

Riva can claim to be Chicago's only waterfront seafood restaurant, with views of the city skyline and Lake Michigan. Though dishes like lobster, king crab, salmon and halibut are popular, Riva also does good steaks in a light and bright smart-casual room.

⊕ H8 ✉ Navy Pier, 700 E. Grand Avenue ☎ 312/644-7482 🕐 Daily lunch and dinner 🚇 Red Line: Grand 🚌 9, 56, 65, 66

ROSEBUD ON RUSH ($$$)

rosebudrestaurants.com

With casual dining and a bar downstairs, as well as a more formal restaurant upstairs, Rosebud serves up huge helpings of Italian fare. Menus may include eggplant parmesan or a daily risotto dish, at this and several other city locations.

⊕ F7 ✉ 720 N. Rush Street ☎ 312/266-6444 🕐 Daily dinner, Mon–Thu "Rush Hour," Sat–Sun brunch 🚇 Red Line: Chicago 🚌 66

SULTAN'S MARKET ($)

chicagofalafel.com

Falafel sandwiches are what this Wicker Park restaurant is known for, but the budget-friendly *shawarma* and other Middle Eastern dishes are also delicious.

⊕ B4 ✉ 2057 W. North Avenue ☎ 773/235-3072 🕐 Mon–Sat 10–10, Sun 10–9 🚇 Blue Line: Damen 🚌 56, 72

XOCO ($–$$)

rickbayless.com

This café/restaurant specializes in Mexican churros, caldos, empanadas and tortas. They also make excellent hot chocolate from the cacao bean.

⊕ D7 ✉ 449 N. Clark Street (enter on Illinois Street) ☎ 312/ 334-3688 🕐 Fri–Sat 8am–10pm, Tue–Thu 8am–9pm 🚇 Brown Line: Chicago 🚌 65

Home to the University of Chicago, the South Side may be the city's most history-rich area but it also looks to the future—it will become the home of former President Barack Obama's presidential library.

Sights   84–91

Walk   92

Entertainment
  and Nightlife 93

Where to Eat   94

Top 25   **TOP 25**

Biking on the Chicago
  Lakefront ▷ 84
DuSable Museum of African
  American History ▷ 85
Hitting a Blues Club ▷ 86
Prairie Avenue District
  ▷ 87
Museum of Science and
  Industry ▷ 88

WEST WASHINGTON BOULEVARD

290 WEST EISENHOWER EXPRESSWAY 290

UNION STATION

Jane Addams Hull-House Museum

University of Illinois Hospital

WEST OGDEN AVENUE

WEST ROOSEVELT ROAD

WEST ROOSEVELT ROAD

University of Illinois at Chicago

Roosevelt Park

National Museum of Mexican Art

SOUTH ASHLAND AVENUE

SOUTH BLUE ISLAND AVE

CHINATOWN

WEST CERMAK ROAD

SOUTH WESTERN AVENUE

SOUTH BLUE ISLAND AVE

5TH DAMEN AVENUE

SOUTH ASHLAND AVENUE

South Branch of Chicago River

55

EXPRESSWAY

McGuane Park

ADLAI E STEVENSON

WEST 31ST STREET

SOUTH ARCHER AVENUE

Armour Square Park

SOUTH HALSTED STREET

DAN RYAN EXPRESSWAY

SOUTH STATE EXPRESSWAY

WEST 35TH STREET

Sox Park

WEST PERSHING ROAD

WEST 43RD STREET

WEST 47TH STREET

90 94

WEST GARFIELD BOULEVARD

0   1 km

0   1 mile

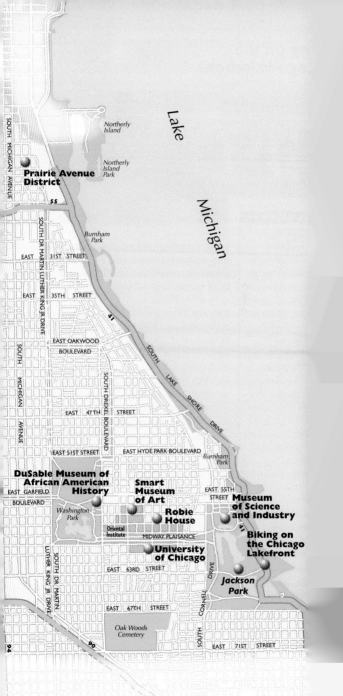

Prairie Avenue District

Lake
Michigan

Northerly Island

Northerly Island Park

SOUTH MICHIGAN AVENUE

55

Burnham Park

EAST 31ST STREET

SOUTH DR MARTIN LUTHER KING JR. DRIVE

EAST 35TH STREET

41

EAST OAKWOOD BOULEVARD

SOUTH DREXEL BOULEVARD

SOUTH MICHIGAN AVENUE

SOUTH LAKE SHORE DRIVE

EAST 47TH STREET

EAST 51ST STREET

EAST HYDE PARK BOULEVARD

Burnham Park

DuSable Museum of African American History

EAST GARFIELD BOULEVARD

Washington Park

Smart Museum of Art

Robie House

EAST 55TH STREET

Museum of Science and Industry

Oriental Institute

MIDWAY PLAISANCE

University of Chicago

Biking on the Chicago Lakefront

EAST 63RD STREET

SOUTH DR MARTIN LUTHER KING JR. DRIVE

SOUTH CORNELL DRIVE

41

Jackson Park

EAST 67TH STREET

Oak Woods Cemetery

SOUTH CORNELL

EAST 71ST STREET

94

90

Biking on the Chicago Lakefront

Bike riding along the lakefront with the city rising in the background

THE BASICS

chicagobicycle.org

✚ See map ▷ 83

✉ Chicago lakefront from Foster Beach on the north to 71st Street on the south

♿ Excellent

❓ Bike and Roll Chicago (bikechicago.com)

✉ Navy Pier, 600 E. Grand Avenue; Millennium Park, 239 E. Randolph Avenue; Riverwalk, 316 N. Wabash Avenue; 53rd Street Bike Center, 1558 E. 53rd Street; North Avenue Beach, 1603 N. Lake Shore Drive; Foster Beach, 5200 N. Lake Shore Drive

☎ 312/729-1000; 866/746-8224

💵 Prices range from $9 per hour to $75 per day, depending on bike; discounts available if booking online

HIGHLIGHTS

● 18 miles (29km) of paths
● 31 beaches
● Concession stands in summer
● Views of the skyline
● Bike rentals

Some 18 miles (29km) of paved paths lure walkers, skaters and cyclists to the lakefront, where the South Side offers busy routes and wonderful views.

Bike city Chicago is very bike-friendly, counting over 200 miles (320km) of bike lanes and closing Lake Shore Drive for one day each summer so that cyclists can enjoy the route exclusively. While the bike lanes on major urban thoroughfares scare the wits of out-of-towners, the lakefront bike path, free of auto traffic, enchant them. North Side routes are popular and weekend crowds jam the lanes around Oak Street Beach. For a quieter pedal, point your handlebars south and cruise past the Museum Campus or to The 606, an elevated bike path through the northwest side neighborhoods. On all paths, the level terrain is beginner-friendly. Numerous bike siteseeing tours are available, including Bobby's Bike Hike and Bike Chicago, with two- to three-hour itineraries devoted to the lakefront, neighborhoods or President Obama's Chicago.

Where to find wheels Divvy Bikes, the light blue rental bikes, can be found all over the city. Rent one for $9.95 a day, and drop it off at any of their 580 locations. Bike Chicago also offers several seasonal rental stands in Chicago. The best located for southbound trips are at Navy Pier or 63rd Street Beach. The "quadcycle," a four-seater vehicle, only looks fun before you find you are pedaling for the entire family.

DuSable Museum of African American History

One of Chicago's unsung museums, this one chronicles aspects of black history, chiefly focusing on African-Americans but also encompassing African and Caribbean cultures.

Settlers The museum is named after Chicago's first permanent settler, Jean Baptiste Point du Sable, a Haitian trader born of a French father and African slave mother in whose home the city's first marriage, election and court decision occurred. Further African-Americans came in three main waves—during the late 19th century and during the two world wars—settling mostly on Chicago's South Side. Black businesses became established, while the expanding community provided the voter base for the first blacks to enter Chicago politics. Among the settlers were many musicians, and what became Chicago blues was born—an electrified urban form of rural blues fused with elements of jazz. The turbulent 1960s saw growing radicalism among Chicago's African-Americans, and the beginning of the rise to national prominence of South Side politician Jesse Jackson.

Exhibits The first-floor rooms display items from the permanent collection, including the Harold Washington Wing, which chronicles the triumph of Chicago's first black mayor in 1983. There are also meticulously planned temporary exhibitions, while the Arts and Crafts Festival, displaying original works on African-American themes, is held on the second weekend of July.

THE BASICS

dusablemuseum.org
➕ See map ▷ 83
✉ 740 E. 56th Place
☎ 773/947-0600
🕐 Tue–Sat 10–5, Sun 12–5
🚇 Red Line: Garfield
🚉 59th Street
🚌 4
♿ Good
💲 Inexpensive; free on Tue

HIGHLIGHTS

● Slavery exhibit, including shackles
● African functional art, including stools and staffs
● Temporary exhibits devoted to black music, art and history
● Craft fair
● Washington Park setting

Hitting a Blues Club

A performer and the audience at Blue Chicago

THE BASICS

Buddy Guy's Legends
▷ 35
B.L.U.E.S. ▷ 76
Velvet Lounge ▷ 93

HIGHLIGHTS

● Buddy Guy's Legends
● Blue Chicago
● B.L.U.E.S.
● Kingston Mines

Southern people moving north in search of jobs in the 1940s amped up the acoustic blues in Chicago, and hearing the music played live is one of the chief attractions of the city.

Blues background Blues music developed among African slaves working southern plantations and descended from "shout outs" of workers in the fields. By the 1920s it developed its signature musical style of repeated three-chord progressions. Vocalists center the genre, but performers regularly improvise solos too. Black America's mass exodus from the rural south to the urban north led many musicians to Chicago. The string bands of the Delta region borrowed from jazz groups in the city, amplifying the sound and adding drums, bass, piano and sometimes horns. Innovators Muddy Waters, B.B. King and Buddy Guy established Chicago's electric style, later widely copied by white players like Elvis Presley. The British rock invasion brought the Rolling Stones and Eric Clapton to town to jam with their blues heroes.

A city with the blues Since 1984, on a weekend in early June, marking the opening of summer, the city stages the Chicago Blues Festival, drawing 750,000 listeners to Grant Park. Admission is free and dedicated fest-goers come early with blankets and coolers to stake out a place on the park lawn. The throng can get fairly boozy by evening, but is all-ages-recommended for most of its duration.

Clarke House exterior (left); main hall in the Glessner House (right)

Prairie Avenue District

After the city burned in the Great Fire of 1871, the wealthy and famous moved to the area around Prairie Avenue on the near South Side, where they built elegant mansions, some now open to tours.

From frontier to fancy Hostile Native Americans attacked European settlers in this district in what became known as the Fort Dearborn Massacre in 1812. Only after the Great Fire wiped out the city did builders reconsider the site. The who's who of Chicago society built here, including the Fields (of Field Museum fame), the Pullmans (luxury Pullman railroad cars) and the Armours (successful meat-packers). Later generations moved north to the Gold Coast, leaving the Prairie Avenue District to decline. By the mid-20th century many houses were razed, arousing the passions of preservationists who saved most of the 11 remaining Victorian mansions.

Two gems Much of the district provides eye candy for passersby, with the exception of two landmarked buildings open for tours. The oldest, the Greek Revival Clarke House, originally owned by hardware dealer Henry B. Clarke, was actually moved to the area from a location farther south. The more unusual Glessner House is a stand-out in rugged granite with a fortress-like presence on a corner. The interior is considerably warmer, home to Arts and Crafts furnishings, a central courtyard and custom-made art.

THE BASICS

✚ F14

✉ 1800 and 1900-blocks of S. Prairie Avenue, 1800-block of S. Indiana, and 211–217 E. Cullerton Street

Glessner House Museum

glessnerhouse.org
Organizes guided tours of Clarke House also.

✉ 1800 S. Prairie Avenue

☎ 312/326-1480

🕐 Tours Wed–Sun at 1 and 3 (limit 15 people, first-come first served)

✋ Free on Wed

Clarke House Museum

🕐 Tours Wed–Sun at 12, 1 and 2 (limit 12 people, first-come, first-served)

🚇 Green, Orange, Red Lines: Roosevelt

🚌 1, 3, 4

♿ Fair

✋ Free; free tours at 1pm and 3pm, Wed, Fri and Sat

HIGHLIGHTS

● Clarke House
● Glessner House
● Self-guided strolls around the Victorian mansions

Museum of Science and Industry

HIGHLIGHTS

- U-505 submarine
- 1936 *Pioneer Zephyr* train
- The Chick Hatchery
- Mirror Maze
- Genetics exhibit
- Apollo 8 Command Module
- Omnimax Theater
- Giant heart

TIP

- To avoid lines on the day, order your tickets in advance via the website and have them held at the will-call window.

You can easily spend a day examining the 35,000 artifacts spread across the museum's 14 acres (5.5ha). Hours will pass like minutes as you discover new things about the world—and beyond— at every turn.

Flying high The first eye-catching item is a Boeing 727 attached to an interior balcony. Packed with multimedia exhibits, the plane simulates a flight from San Francisco to Chicago, making full use of flaps, rudders and undercarriage. Other flight-related exhibits include a simulated mission aboard a naval F-14 fighter. Reflecting other modes of transportation are the 500mph (804kph) *Spirit of America* car, a walk-through 1944 German U-boat and the Apollo 8 spacecraft. The

Clockwise from left: Robot exhibit; Exterior of the Museum of Science and Industry; Pioneer Zephyr; the U-505 exhibit—the conning tower; a demonstration in the control room of the U505 exhibit

moon-circling Apollo craft forms just a small part of the excellent Henry Crown Space Center, housed in an adjoining building.

Medical matters A giant heart that beats to the rhythm of your pulse is among exhibits detailing the workings of the human body. It's Part of You! The Experience is a multi-faceted exhibit examining the link between the mind, body and spirit. Play Mindball, a relaxation game, and see how your face will age based on your habits and lifestyle.

Industrial issues MSI re-creates a coal mine, complete with a simulated descent to 600ft (180m) in a miners' car. The Farm exhibit allows you to "get into" a John Deere combine harvester to virtually harvest a cornfield.

THE BASICS

msichicago.org
➕ See map ▷ 83
✉ 5700 Lake Shore Drive
☎ 773/684-1414
🕐 Daily 9.30–4
🍴 Several cafés
🚇 Red Line: Garfield
🚌 55th, 56th, 57th streets
🚍 6, 10
♿ Excellent
💰 Moderate; see website for free days schedule; separate charge for Omnimax Theater

More to See

CHINATOWN

chicagochinatown.org

The ornate Chinatown Gate arching over Cermak at Wentworth marks the heart of Chinatown. Chicago's oldest Chinese district was founded by 19th-century railroad workers. Perhaps the most atmospheric of Chicago's many ethnic enclaves, Chinatown is popular for its many restaurants and streets of stores selling Asian gifts, decorative items, cooking utensils and foods.

➕ D15 🚇 Red Line: Cermak/Chinatown 🚌 24, 62

JACKSON PARK

In 1893, 27 million people attended the World's Columbian Exposition, in what became Jackson Park, now a fantastic green space with sports courts, a Japanese garden and the Museum of Science and Industry (▷ 88). This will become the home of the Barack Obama Presidential Library and Museum, which is planned to open in 2020.

➕ See map ▷ 83 ✉ 6401 S. Stony Island Avenue (between S. Stony Island Avenue and Lake Michigan) 🚇 Red Line: Garfield 🚆 55th, 56th, 57th streets 🚌 6, 10

JANE ADDAMS HULL-HOUSE MUSEUM

uic.edu/jaddams/hull/hull_house.html

In the late 19th century Jane Addams created Hull House, a center in one of the neediest neighborhoods offering English-language and US citizenship courses, child care and other services. An entertaining 15-minute slide show tells the story. The rooms of the main building are lined with memorabilia.

➕ C11 ✉ 800 S. Halsted Street ☎ 312/413-5353 🕐 Tue–Fri 10–4, Sun 12–4 🚇 Blue Line: UIC-Halsted 🚆 Halsted 🚌 8 ♿ Fair 🎟 Free

NATIONAL MUSEUM OF MEXICAN ART

nationalmuseumofmexicanart.org

Explore Mexican culture through this collection of 6,000 works by

Japanese Gardens in Jackson Park

artists of Mexican nationality or descent. Exhibits include prints, photography, paintings and sculpture.

🔲 See map ▷ 82 ✉ 1852 W. 19th Street ☎ 312/738-1503 🕐 Tue–Sun 10–5 🚇 Pink Line: 18th Street 🚌 50 ♿ Good 💲 Free

ROBIE HOUSE
flwright.org/visit/robiehouse

A famed example of Frank Lloyd Wright's Prairie School style of architecture, the Frederick C. Robie House was built in 1910. The horizontal emphasis reflects the Midwest's open spaces. Wright designed not only the structure, but all of the interiors and fixtures. Highlights include cantilevered roof eaves and continuous bands of art-glass windows. The museum shop offers a wide variety of items, from pens to furniture.

🔲 See map ▷ 83 ✉ 5757 S. Woodlawn Avenue ☎ 312/994-4000; tickets 800/514-3849 🕐 Thu–Mon 10.30–3 🚇 Green Line: Cottage Grove 🚉 59th Street 🚌 4 ♿ Few 💲 Moderate

SMART MUSEUM OF ART
smartmuseum.uchicago.edu

With more than 10,000 objects, strong in postwar Chicago art, Japanese painting and contemporary Chinese photography, this museum is a hidden gem, which introduces lesser-known facets of art history and encourages comparisons between different cultures—from Asia to Europe.

🔲 See map ▷ 83 ✉ 5550 S. Greenwood Avenue ☎ 773/702-0200 🕐 Tue–Sun 10–5 (till 8pm Thu) 🚇 Green Line: Garfield 🚌 55 💲 Free

UNIVERSITY OF CHICAGO
uchicago.edu

The oldest buildings on the leafy campus are in English Gothic style, but modernists Eero Saarinen and Ludwig Mies van der Rohe added boxier structures in the 1950s and '60s.

🔲 See map ▷ 83 ✉ Campus is largely bounded by Blackstone Avenue, Cottage Grove, 55th Street and 59th Street 🚇 Green Line: Garfield 🚌 55, 170, 171, 172

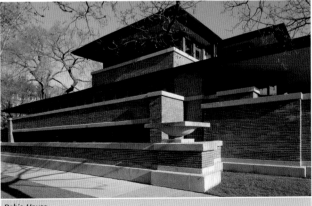

Robie House

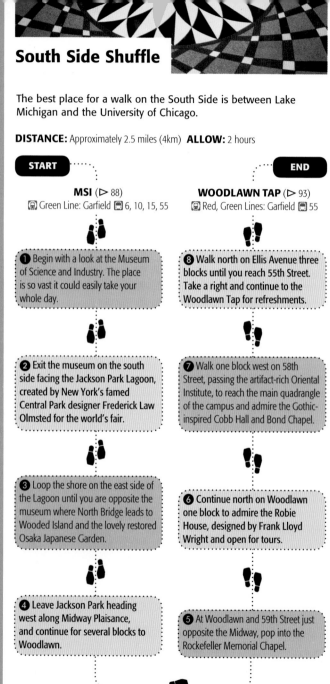

South Side Shuffle

The best place for a walk on the South Side is between Lake Michigan and the University of Chicago.

DISTANCE: Approximately 2.5 miles (4km) **ALLOW:** 2 hours

START

MSI (▷ 88)
Ⓜ Green Line: Garfield 🚌 6, 10, 15, 55

END

WOODLAWN TAP (▷ 93)
Ⓜ Red, Green Lines: Garfield 🚌 55

❶ Begin with a look at the Museum of Science and Industry. The place is so vast it could easily take your whole day.

❷ Exit the museum on the south side facing the Jackson Park Lagoon, created by New York's famed Central Park designer Frederick Law Olmsted for the world's fair.

❸ Loop the shore on the east side of the Lagoon until you are opposite the museum where North Bridge leads to Wooded Island and the lovely restored Osaka Japanese Garden.

❹ Leave Jackson Park heading west along Midway Plaisance, and continue for several blocks to Woodlawn.

❺ At Woodlawn and 59th Street just opposite the Midway, pop into the Rockefeller Memorial Chapel.

❻ Continue north on Woodlawn one block to admire the Robie House, designed by Frank Lloyd Wright and open for tours.

❼ Walk one block west on 58th Street, passing the artifact-rich Oriental Institute, to reach the main quadrangle of the campus and admire the Gothic-inspired Cobb Hall and Bond Chapel.

❽ Walk north on Ellis Avenue three blocks until you reach 55th Street. Take a right and continue to the Woodlawn Tap for refreshments.

SOUTH SIDE WALK

COURT THEATRE

courttheatre.org

The University of Chicago's theater has been staging high-quality dramas and musicals for more than 50 years. Noted for its fine acting and innovative staging, the Court deserves the attention more easily snared by downtown and North Side troops.

✉ 5535 W. Ellis Avenue ☎ 773/753-4472
🚊 Green Line: Garfield 🚌 55

OMNIMAX THEATER

msichicago.org

A curving, five-story screen embedded with 72 speakers shows large-format IMAX movies on subjects both scientific and entertaining in a separate building attached to the Museum of Science and Industry.

✉ 57th Street and Lake Shore Drive
☎ 773/684-1414 🚊 Green Line: Garfield
🚌 6, 10, 15, 55

THE PROMONTORY

promontorychicago.com

Dance or just sit and listen to the live soul, jazz, afro fusion, hip-hop, and other black-rooted music in this popular bar. Tickets are needed for some shows. Check out the wall of vinyl albums in the entrance, signed by the artists who have performed there.

✉ 5311 S. Lake Park Avenue West
☎ 312/801-2100 🚊 51st/53rd Hyde Park
🚌 2, 6

REGGIE'S CHICAGO

reggieslive.com

Reggie's Music Joint is a bar and grill that also puts on a full range of live music, from punk and indie to home-grown Chicago jazz and blues. There's also a menu of salads, sandwiches, burgers and TV dinners—served just like the TV dinners of old, on a silver foil tray. There are 25 draft beers too, even more by the bottle, and nearby at 2109 S. State is Reggie's Rock Club, if you just want music and no food.

✉ 2105 S. State Street ☎ 312/949-0120
🚊 Red Line: Cermak/Chinatown 🚌 21, 29

VELVET LOUNGE

velvetloungechicago.com

Chicago saxophonist Fred Anderson runs one of the city's most revered jazz listening rooms. The original was destroyed to make way for housing but the club survived and thrives at its new location, and attracts the city's best players on the calendar.

✉ 67 E. Cermak Road ☎ 312/794-5904
🚊 Red Line: Cermak 🚌 21, 29

WOODLAWN TAP

Chicago is famed for its neighborhood taverns, corner taps that serve as places where communities gather and bind. Hyde Park lacks the saloons of other neighborhoods, but the Woodlawn Tap, also known as "Jimmy's," goes a long way to fill in, with three dimly lit rooms filled with academics and studious types deep in conversation.

✉ 1172 E. 55th Street ☎ 773/643-5516
🚊 Red, Green Lines: Garfield 🚌 55

CHINESE NEW YEAR

At the end of January thousands of visitors flock to Chinatown to celebrate Chinese New Year. The parade features dragon dancers, martial artists and Chinese dancers as well as the incongruous bagpipe marching band and assorted politicians. The route runs through the heart of the neighborhood on Wentworth from Cermak to 24th Street. Afterward parade-goers jam the area's many restaurants for dim sum.

SOUTH SIDE ENTERTAINMENT AND NIGHTLIFE

Where to Eat

PRICES
Prices are approximate, based on a 3-course meal for one person.
$$$$ over $50
$$$ $31–$50
$$ $16–$30
$ up to $15

CHICAGO'S HOME OF CHICKEN AND WAFFLES ($)

chicagoschickenandwaffles.com

Whether it's a late-night feast or an after-church breakfast, people crave the soul food at this Bronzeville spot. While they're best known for their fried chicken and waffles, fans also rave about the Sunday breakfast.

✉ 3947 S. King Drive ☎ 773/536-3300 🕐 Daily breakfast, lunch and dinner 🚇 Green Line: Indiana 🚌 3

EMPEROR'S CHOICE ($$)

chicagoemperorschoice.com

At this intimate restaurant, portraits of former Chinese emperors hang above diners who are feasting on some of Chinatown's most creative seafood dishes. For a special occasion order the Peking duck—but you'll need to place your order a day in advance.

✉ 2238 S. Wentworth Avenue ☎ 312/225-8800 🕐 Daily lunch and dinner 🚇 Red Line: Cermak/Chinatown 🚌 24

FLO & SANTOS ($–$$)

floandsantos.com

The menu at this informal restaurant mixes Italian and Polish favorites, sometimes in the same dish. The specialty pizzas are excellent too.

✉ 1310 S. Wabash Avenue ☎ 312/566-9817 🕐 Daily lunch and dinner; from 9am on Chicago Bear game days 🚇 Red, Orange, Green Lines: Roosevelt 🚌 4

GIOCO ($$–$$$)

gioco-chicago.com

Fine Italian menu combining pizzas, homemade pasta and roast meats served in a former speakeasy.

✉ 1312 S. Wabash Avenue ☎ 312/939-3870 🕐 Closed Sat and Sun lunch 🚇 Red, Orange, Green Lines: Roosevelt 🚌 4

LA PETITE FOLIE ($$$)

lapetitefolie.com

A rare, fine-dining outpost in Hyde Park, La Petite Folie serves unfussy French food. It's a popular precurtain spot for Court Theatre patrons.

✉ 1504 E. 55th Street ☎ 773/493-1394 🕐 No lunch Sat–Sun; closed Mon 🚇 Green Line: Garfield 🚌 55

MANNY'S DELI & CAFETERIA ($)

Mannysdeli.com

Corned beef and pastrami sandwiches are piled high, with a potato pancake and pickle on the side, at this landmark Jewish deli. Grab a tray and move down the cafeteria line, possibly picking a slice of cherry pie that is President Barack Obama's favorite.

✉ 1141 S. Jefferson Street ☎ 312/939-2855 🕐 Tue–Sat 7am–8pm, Mon 7–3, Sun 8–3 🚇 Green Line: Garfield 🚌 55

PHOENIX ($$)

chinatownphoenix.com

This popular Chinatown restaurant serves up panoramic views of the Chicago skyline from picture windows, along with a lively dim sum trade. Many of the waiters do not speak English; good humor and the pointing method of ordering prevail. Long waits are common on weekends.

✉ 2131 S. Archer Avenue ☎ 312/328-0848 🕐 Daily lunch and dinner 🚇 Red Line: Cermak 🚌 21, 24

Ironically one of the top tourist sights isn't even in the city. Frank Lloyd Wright's home and original office is in Oak Park. Some 198 neighborhoods aim to lure you, particularly Wicker Park and Bucktown.

Sights	98–102	Top 25	TOP 25
Shopping	103	Boutique Browsing in Wicker Park/Bucktown ▷ 99	
Entertainment and Nightlife	104	Frank Lloyd Wright Home and Studio ▷ 100	
Where to Eat	106	Wrigley Field ▷ 101	

AVENUE

NORTH

WESTERN

NORTH

14

41

Loyola University,
Lake Shore

AVENUE

ASHLAND

PARK

ROAD

WEST   IRVING

**Graceland
Cemetery
and
Arboretum**

Wrigley Field

Boystown

41

AVENUE

Chicago River North Branch

90

94

Lincoln
Park

Montrose
Harbor

NORTH LAKE SHORE DRIVE

Lake

Michigan

Belmont
Harbor

North
Pond

Diversey
Harbor

Lincoln
Park

South
Pond

**Wicker Park /
Bucktown Boutique
Browsing**

OLD
TOWN
CHICAGO

Union
Park

Chicago   River

290

LOOP

WEST   ROOSEVELT   ROAD

Grant
Park

Burnham Park
Harbor

SOUTH

55

SOUTH

SOUTH

HALSTED

DAN

90

RYAN

94

EXPRESSWAY

STREET

SOUTH

MICHIGAN

41

SOUTH LAKE SHORE DRIVE

31st Street
Harbor

McKinley
Park

SOUTH

WESTERN

ASHLAND

AVENUE

WEST

Sherman
Park

GARFIELD   BOULEVARD

EAST   47TH STREET

AVENUE

Washington
Park

BOULEVARD

Gage
Park

WEST

63RD   STREET

Ogden
Park

90

94

41

Jackson
Park

Interiors of Stitch (opposite); P45 (left); City Soles (right)

Boutique Browsing in Wicker Park/Bucktown

West of the Gold Coast, following North Avenue, a progressive, urban neighborhood emerges. This gentrifying area is a hub for artists and musicians, and contains many new restaurants and a growing range of shops. Festivals and a farmers' market bring in crowds from spring through fall.

History In the mid-1850s Irish immigrants settled around the Rolling Mill Steel Works. Businesses lined the commercial avenues and homes were tucked in streets behind them. After the Great Fire of 1871 the area boomed as the well-heeled built spacious Victorian mansions. Waves of immigration followed, running along Milwaukee Avenue. From the 1930s to the 1970s the area declined, but in the 1980s Wicker Park and Bucktown took off as shops, nightclubs and restaurants all moved in.

Where to shop There is so much choice here. Both vintage and on-trend fashions are on show at the boutique Ragstock (1433 N. Milwaukee Avenue). P45 (1643 N. Damen Avenue) sells cutting-edge women's clothing from emerging American designers. High-quality, American-made denim clothes are designed with a California flare at Current/Elliott (1723 N. Damen Ave). Pagoda Red (1714 N. Damen Avenue) imports antiques from Asia, from Chinese cabinets to fans. Stitch (1723 N. Damen Avenue) is the place for accessories, City Soles (2001 North Avenue) for shoes.

THE BASICS

wickerparkbucktown.com
🔁 See map ▷ 97
✉ The center of the neighborhood is at the three-way intersection of Milwaukee, Damen and North avenues
🕐 Most shops Mon–Sat 11–7, Sun 12–5
🚇 Blue Line: Damen
🚌 50, 70, 72

HIGHLIGHTS

- P45
- Current/Elliott
- Pagoda Red
- Stitch
- City Soles

Frank Lloyd Wright Home and Studio

The Children's Playroom inside the house (left); the exterior of Frank Lloyd Wright's Studio (right)

THE BASICS

flwright.org
➕ See map ▷ 96
✉ 951 Chicago Avenue, Oak Park
☎ 312/994-4000
🕐 Guided tours only: daily 10–4 Mar–Dec; 10–3 Jan–Feb
🚆 Green Line: Oak Park Avenue
🚉 Oak Park
🚌 23
♿ Few
💲 Moderate

HIGHLIGHTS

● Barrel-vaulted playroom
● Drafting Room with chain harness system to support the roof
● Stained-glass leaded windows
● Skylights
● Wright-designed furniture

TIP

● Advanced tickets are highly recommended. Get them up to midnight the night before the tour from the website or call Etix
☎ 800/514-3849.

The Frank Lloyd Wright Home and Studio provides an insight into the early ideas of one of the greatest and most influential architects of the 20th century.

Organic ideas Working for the Chicago-based architect Louis Sullivan, the 22-year-old Frank Lloyd Wright designed this home in 1889 for himself, his first wife and their children, and furnished it with pieces he designed. The shingled exterior is not typical of Wright, but the bold geometric shape stands out among the neighboring Queen Anne-style houses. Inside, the open-plan, central fireplaces and low ceilings are the earliest examples of the elements that became fundamental in Wright's so-called Prairie School of Architecture. Particularly notable are the children's playroom, the high-backed chairs in the dining room and the willow tree that grows through the walls in keeping with Wright's theory of organic architecture— architecture in harmony with its surroundings.

Prairie views In 1893, Wright opened his own practice in an annex to the house: A concealed entrance leads into an office showcasing many of Wright's ideas, such as suspended lamps and an open-plan work space. The draftsmen once employed here on seminal Prairie School buildings worked in a stunningly designed room in sight of what was then prairie. Lloyd Wright's disciples designed 125 buildings here, including the nearby Unity Temple and the Robie House in Hyde Park on Chicago's South Side.

Aerial view of Wrigley Field (left); a large red sign welcomes fans to the ballpark (right)

Wrigley Field

Loyal Chicago Cub fans were finally rewarded for their patience with a World Series Championship in 2016—their first in 108 years. Their home field is an integral part of the team's identity, and a beloved landmark in Chicago.

Landmark With its ivy-covered brick outfield wall, Wrigley Field provides the perfect setting for America's traditional pastime. Built in 1914, the stadium has steadily resisted artificial turf, and the game takes place on grass within an otherwise ordinary city neighborhood, now known as Wrigleyville. With insufficient car-parking space, most spectators have to endure densely packed El trains to reach the ballpark. General admission bleacher seating overlooking the outfield is popular at Wrigley. Dedicated Cubs fans withstand the vagaries of Chicago weather, which during the April to October season can encompass anything from snow to sunshine and 100°F (38°C) temperatures.

Tradition Above the seats is the much-loved 1937 scoreboard on which the numbers are moved not by computer but by human hands. Fans stand in the middle of the seventh inning and sing "Take Me Out to the Ballgame," often led by a visiting celebrity and accompanied by a live organist. Modern day to Wrigley Field include two huge video boards showing replays, statistics and team history. Rooftops across the street from the ballpark have been converted in to clubs for fans to watch the game.

THE BASICS

chicago.cubs.mlb.com

⊕ See map ▷ 97

✉ 1060 W. Addison Street

☎ 773/404-2827

🕐 Games: Apr–early Oct

🍴 Fast-food stands; three restaurants

🚇 Red Line: Addison

🚌 22, 152

♿ Good

🎟 Tickets moderate to expensive

HIGHLIGHTS

● Outfield wall ivy
● Bleacher seats
● Glimpsing the game from the Addison El stop
● Hand-operated scoreboard
● Seventh inning stretch

More to See

THE 606

the606.org

This exciting 2.7-mile (4.3km) elevated bike path takes you over streets, past houses and parks and through the Northwestside neighborhoods. With lots of on/off ramps, it's easy to stop and sample the area's shops and cafés. Bike rentals are at each end of the path.

➕ See map ▷ 96–97 ✉ Bloomingdale Road, between Ashland and Ridgeway
◉ Daily 6am–11pm 🚇 Blue Line: Western, Damen 🚌 X49, 50

BOYSTOWN

northalsted.com

The pocket of Lakeview around North Halsted Street from Belmont north to Addison is the focus of the LGBT community in Chicago, and has a collection of bars and some good restaurants.

➕ See map ▷ 97 ✉ Halsted Street from Belmont north to Addison 🚇 Red Line: Belmont Addison; Brown Line: Belmont
🚌 8, 77 ♿ Good

ERNEST HEMINGWAY MUSEUM

ehfop.org

A collection remembering the Nobel Prize-winning writer who spent his first 18 years in Oak Park. Hemingway's birthplace, at 339 N. Oak Park Avenue, is open when the museum is.

➕ See map ▷ 96 ✉ 200 N. Oak Park Avenue ☎ 708/524–5383 ◉ Sat 10–5, Fri and Sun 1–5 🚇 Green Line: Oak Park
🚆 Oak Park 🚌 23 ♿ Few 💵 Inexpensive

FRANK LLOYD WRIGHT TOUR

flwright.org

The lovely Oak Park neighborhood surrounding the Lloyd Wright's former home and studio hosts 26 Wright-designed homes, and is the largest concentration of the architect's buildings anywhere in the world. The Wright Foundation rents headsets for the self-guided Historic Neighborhood walking tours (see flwright.org). Take the tour after visiting the Frank Lloyd Wright Home and Studio (▷ 100), which will familiarize you with the Prairie School style.

➕ See map ▷ 96 ✉ Oak Park
☎ 708/848-1976 🚇 Green Line: Oak Park Avenue 🚌 23 ♿ Few 💵 Moderate

GARFIELD PARK CONSERVATORY

garfield-conservatory.org

The conservatory has 5 acres (2ha) of tropical and subtropical plants. Highlights include collections of palms, ferns and cacti. Chicagoans come here for gardening tips and for shows.

➕ See map ▷ 96 ✉ 300 N. Central Park Avenue ☎ 312/746-5100 ◉ Sun-Tue, Thu–Sat 9–5, Wed 9–8. Extended hours for shows 🚇 Green Line: Conservatory/Central Park 🚌 82 ♿ Few 💵 Free

GRACELAND CEMETERY AND ARBORETUM

gracelandcemetery.org

Covering some 120 acres (50ha), Graceland is the resting place of famous and infamous Chicagoans. Louis Sullivan is here, as are other Chicago architects. The free map from the office is essential.

➕ See map ▷ 97 ✉ 4001 N. Clark Street
☎ 773/525-1105 ◉ Mon–Fri 8–4, Sat–Sun 9–4 (until 6 daily in summer) 🚇 Brown Line: Irving Park; Red Line: Sheridan 🚌 80
♿ Good 💵 Free

THE ALLEY

thealleychicago.com

If your idea of an accessory is a classic Zippo lighter or a Che Guevara belt buckle, the Alley stores, alternative clothing stockists, is the place to find it, plus leather jackets and motorcycle boots.

✉ 2620 W. Fletcher Street ☎ 773/404-8000
🚇 Brown, Red Lines: Belmont 🚌 22, 36

BEATNIX

Packed from floor to ceiling, this stash of wild and unbelievable attire is like Disneyland for the daring.

✉ 3400 N. Halsted Avenue ☎ 773/281-6933
🚇 Brown, Red Lines: Belmont 🚌 152

BELMONT ARMY SURPLUS

belmontarmy.wordpress.com

This former army surplus store has expanded over three floors to become a top Chicago spot for hiking boots, backpacks and more.

✉ 855 W. Belmont Avenue ☎ 773/549-1038
🚇 Brown, Red Lines: Belmont 🚌 77

THE BOOK TABLE

booktable.net

This independent bookstore carries over 60,000 discounted new and used titles. The stock is especially strong in art, architecture, history and children's books, but there is plenty of reading material here for all interests.

✉ 1045 Lake Street, Oak Park ☎ 708/386-9800 🚇 Green Line: Harlem

BROADWAY ANTIQUES MARKET

bamchicago.com

The 75-plus antique dealers at this two-floor antiques haven sell everything from art deco to mid-20th-century modern pieces.

✉ 6130 N. Broadway Avenue ☎ 773/743-5444 🚇 Red Line: Granville 🚌 136

DSW SHOE WAREHOUSE

dswshoe.com

Whether in need of a pair of designer shoes for a top night out or simply solid footwear for exploring the city's top sights, this long-established outlet is the place to find them.

✉ 3131 N. Clark Street ☎ 773/975-7182
🚇 Brown, Red Lines: Belmont 🚌 77

LE THRIFT CONSIGNMENT BOUTIQUE

LeThrift.com

The boutique sells high-end designer clothing for women from brands such as Prada, Chanel and Tory Burch and top quality vintage accessories and clothing, so this is the place to add top-name designers to your wardrobe at bargain prices.

✉ 2128 W. Belmont Street ☎ 312/912-9676
🚇 Green Line: Oak Park; Blue Line: Division
🚌 23

SAINT ALFRED

stalfred.com

A small store, Saint Alfred features men's and women's footwear and sneakers (tennies) from many different brands, as well as men's and women's casual sport clothing.

✉ 1531 N. Milwaukee Avenue ☎ 773/486-7159 🚇 Blue Line: Damen 🚌 56

UNABRIDGED BOOKSTORE

unabridgedbookstore.com

Chicago's leading LGBT bookstore and a rare independent bookseller offers publications on a wide array of topics. Well-read and knowledgable employees offer their personal touts for books they like, so look out for their notes attached to the racks.

✉ 3251 N. Broadway ☎ 773/883-9119
🚇 Red Line: Belmont 🚌 36, 77

Entertainment and Nightlife

BEAT KITCHEN

beatkitchen.com

A smallish but popular venue, the Beat Kitchen makes a good setting for folk and rock acts, predominantly from around Chicago.

✉ 2100 W. Belmont Avenue ☎ 773/281-4444 🚇 Brown, Red Lines: Belmont 🚌 22

CUBBY BEAR

cubbybear.com

Its location opposite Wrigley Field makes this sports bar a favorite spot for post-Cub games. The live music spans rock, country, reggae and blues, plus dancing and beer.

✉ 1059 W. Addison Street ☎ 773/327-1662 🚇 Brown Line: Addison 🚌 22, 152

GREEN MILL COCKTAIL LOUNGE

greenmilljazz.com

Classic Uptown jazz club that dates back to Chicago's Prohibition days as a speakeasy. Home of the Sunday night Uptown Poetry Slam, an open-mic night for performance poets that has spawned imitators the world over.

✉ 4802 N. Broadway Avenue ☎ 773/878-5552 🚇 Red Line: Lawrence 🚌 36

MARTYRS

martyrslive.com

A showcase place for up-and-coming musicians and comedians, there's always a fun live show going on at this bar, a favorite among locals.

✉ 3855 N. Lincoln Avenue ☎ 773/404-9494 🚇 Brown Line: Irving Park 🚌 11

METRO

metrochicago.com

Major mid-size venue for live rock, with ample space for dancing and plentiful seating with good views. Other levels have a nightclub and coffee bar.

RAVINIA FESTIVAL

From mid-June to Labor Day, the northern suburb of Highland Park plays host to the Ravinia Festival. The summer home of the Chicago Symphony Orchestra, Ravinia also stages rock and jazz concerts, dance events and other cultural activities. Chartered buses ferry festival goers the 25 miles (40km) from central Chicago; you can also get there by commuter train. Details ☎ 847/433–8819; ravinia.org.

✉ 3730 N. Clark Street ☎ 773/549-4140 🚇 Brown Line: Addison 🚌 22, 152

MUSIC BOX THEATRE

musicboxtheatre.com

Independent, classic and foreign films fill the slate at this 1929 Lakeview movie palace with twinkling stars in the ceiling and an organ employed during holiday sing-alongs.

✉ 3733 N. Southport Avenue ☎ 773/871-6604 🚇 Brown Line: Southport 🚌 9, 77, 80

OLD TOWN SCHOOL OF FOLK MUSIC

oldtownschool.org

Set in "restaurant row" of the Lincoln Square neighborhood, this folk and world music venue hosts concerts in an intimate setting. The school also offers music lessons with instruments ranging from the ukelele to Qi Gong (chi kung).

✉ 4544 N. Lincoln Avenue ☎ 773/728-6000 🚇 Brown Line: Western 🚌 11, 49

THE WILD HARE

wildharemusic.com

Top-notch live reggae and other Caribbean and African sounds in the heart of Wrigleyville.

✉ 2610 N. Halsted Street ☎ 773/770-3511 🚇 Brown, Purple, Red Lines: Fullerton

Where to Eat

PRICES

Prices are approximate, based on a
3-course meal for one person.

$$$$ over $50
$$$ $31–$50
$$ $16–$30
$ up to $15

ARUN'S ($$$$)

arunsthai.com

Superb Thai fare, with subtle spicing
reflecting the exceptional talent in the
kitchen. Tasting menus only.

✉ 4156 N. Kedzie Avenue ☎ 773/539-1909
🕐 Dinner only; closed Mon 🚇 Brown Line:
Kedzie 🚌 80, 82

BARBAKAN RESTAURANT ($)

barbakanrestaurant.com

Unprepossessing interior, complete with
aging formica tables, conceals delicious
Polish food at low prices; the soup
options change daily. Innovative "meal
passes" can be purchased for $55.

✉ 3145 N. Central Avenue ☎ 773/202-8181
🕐 Daily lunch and dinner 🚇 Blue Line:
Belmont 🚌 85

BISTRO CAMPAGNE ($$$)

bistrocampagne.com

Intimate setting for quality French
cuisine from a small but well-chosen
menu; come early in the week to avoid
the crowds. Outdoor dining in summer
in a pleasant garden.

✉ 4518 N. Lincoln Avenue ☎ 773/271-6100
🕐 Dinner only; Sun brunch 🚇 Brown Line:
Western 🚌 11, 49, 78

CHICAGO BRAUHAUS
($$–$$$)

chicagobrauhaus.com

Over the years Chicago has lost many
of its famed German restaurants. The

40-plus-year-old Brauhaus proudly
waves the flag with a menu of plentiful
standards like schnitzel and sausage and
frothy beers on tap. The house oompah
band gets dancers to their feet.

✉ 4732 N. Lincoln Avenue ☎ 773/784-4444
🕐 No lunch Sat; closed Tue 🚇 Brown Line:
Western 🚌 11, 4

CLUB LUCKY ($–$$)

clubluckychicago.com

The Italian menu is long at this lively
neighborhood supper club in Bucktown,
though the food takes second place to
the socializing.

➕ A4 ✉ 1824 W. Wabansia Street
☎ 773/227-2300 🕐 Dinner only weekends
🚇 Blue Line: Damon 🚌 7

NOON-O-KABAB ($$)

noonokabab.com

Feast on the large, budget-friendly
portions of fresh, authentic Persian
food at this homey restaurant, in one
of Chicago's Middle Eastern neighborhoods. Specialties include their seasonal
kebabs, warm pitta bread, char-boiled
vegetables and dill rice.

➕ A4 ✉ 4661 N. Kedzie Avenue
☎ 773/279-9309 🕐 Dinner only weekends
🚇 Brown Line: Kedzie 🚌 22, 49, 67, 77

INDIA IN CHICAGO

Chicago's Indian community thrives along
Devon Avenue on the far North Side of the
city. Bollywood video stores and sari shops
occasionally intersperse the long string of
restaurants that line either side of the street
west of Western Avenue. Top choices
include Tiffin (✉ 2536 W. Devon Avenue
☎ 773/338-2143) and Hema's Kitchen
(✉ 2439 W. Devon Avenue ☎ 773/338-
1627). Many places feature a bargain-price
buffet for the midday meal.

Chicago's hotels are largely clustered downtown within walking distance of shopping, restaurants, nightlife and museums. Lodgings near to O'Hare Airport cater primarily to business travelers.

Introduction   108

Budget Hotels   109

Mid-Range Hotels   110–111

Luxury Hotels   112

Introduction

Chicago's hotels concentrate in the tourist regions downtown, but within that region, where you stay depends very much on what you aim to do.

An Experience
If it's shopping you seek, look for something on the near North Side or along the Magnificent Mile. Loop district hotels plant you closest to many top cultural attractions, including the Art Institute of Chicago and Randolph Street theaters. River North hotels provide great access to restaurants and nightlife. To experience life as a Chicago resident you might try something in close proximity to Wrigley Field or the Lincoln Park Zoo.

For Your Own Budget
Most of the city's luxury hotels, including the Trump Tower, Park Hyatt and Peninsula, are on or near the Magnificent Mile, offering easy access to high-end shops. Mid-range hotels are scattered throughout the Loop, River North and near North Side regions. Budget hotels tend to be pushed to the margins of downtown or in North Side neighborhoods such as Lakeview.

Best Times to Visit
Because business travel traffic is so vital to hoteliers, many of them drop their rates to lure in weekend guests. You probably won't find such bargains in the height of summer, but during the off-season the sales can be dramatic.

DATES TO AVOID

Chicago has the biggest convention center in the country, McCormick Place. Some conventions swell to take every hotel room in the region. Others, such as the National Restaurant Show each May, make getting a restaurant reservation difficult. Business travelers account for 55 percent of hotel business downtown. September, October, November and May are big convention months. If crowds concern you, phone ahead when booking your hotel and ask about group business during your stay.

Budget Hotels

BEST WESTERN HAWTHORNE TERRACE

hawthorneterrace.com

Wrigley Field is a short walk from this 59-room neighborhood inn with nice-for-the-price amenities including WiFi and a fitness center. Also close to Wrigleyville and North Halsted restaurant scene, as well as the Lincoln Park lakefront.

➕ Off map at C1 ✉ 3434 N. Broadway ☎ 888/860-3400 🚇 Red Line: Addison 🚌 36

CITY SUITES HOTEL

cityinns.com

Most of the 45 rooms are suites—and represent good value. You will certainly feel that you are at the heart of the action here as the lively, and rather loud, shopping and nightlife strip is right on the hotel's doorstep.

➕ Off map at C1 ✉ 933 W. Belmont Avenue ☎ 773/404-3400; 800/248-9108 🚇 Brown, Red Lines: Belmont 🚌 77

DAYS INN CHICAGO— LINCOLN PARK

daysinnchicago.net

Near the lakefront but 3 miles (5km) north of the Loop is this simple but pleasant hotel where room prices include a continental breakfast. The hotel is on a busy street intersection and is surrounded by restaurants and shopping, and there are train and bus stops close by.

➕ Off map ✉ 644 W. Diversey ☎ 773/525-7010 🚇 Red Line: Fullerton and Wellington 🚌 22, 76

OHIO HOUSE

ohiohousemotel.com

This dependable, simple motel has 50 rooms and offers exceptionally good rates in a River North location. Free parking and WiFi.

➕ E8 ✉ 600 N. LaSalle Street ☎ 312/943-6000; 866/601-6446 🚇 Red Line: Grand 🚌 37, 41

RED ROOF INN CHICAGO DOWNTOWN

redroofinndowntownchicago.com

Rooms are small but well planned in a historic building, some with mini-refrigerator and microwave. The location can't be beat at this price, two blocks off Michigan Avenue in the bustling and usually high-price Streeterville district.

➕ F8 ✉ 162 E. Ontario Street ☎ 312/787-3580 🚇 Red Line: Grand 🚌 65, 157

WILLOWS HOTEL

willowshotelchicago.com

A hotel with 55 great-value rooms, close to the lake, Lincoln Park and numerous bars and restaurants. The building dates from the 1920s and is full of character—the lobby is especially charming, with a fireplace and high windows.

➕ Off map at D1 ✉ 555 W. Surf Street ☎ 773/528-8400; 800/787-3108 🚇 Brown Line: Diversey 🚌 36

B&BS
Bed-and-breakfasts are typically Victorian homes fitted out in sumptuous style and filled with antiques. They span all price categories and there is a particularly strong concentration in Oak Park. Chicago Bed and Breakfast Association (Chicago-bed-breakfast.com) operates a reservation system; it handles properties that are usually centrally located.

WHERE TO STAY BUDGET HOTELS

Mid-Range Hotels

ACME HOTEL

acmehotelcompany.com

Filled with modern pop art, this boutique hotel seems more expensive than it is, especially for a downtown hotel. Hi-tech amenities and check-ins appeal to young travelers, and so does their new ski lodge-like bar with a hot tub.

⊞ F8 ⊠ 15 E. Ohio Street ☎ 312/894-0800 🚇 Red Line: Grand 🚌 36

COURTYARD BY MARRIOTT

marriott.com

The Loop is adjacent to this Marriott hotel so, unsurprisingly, the 337 comfortable, large rooms here are very popular with business travelers.

⊞ F8 ⊠ 30 E. Hubbard Street ☎ 312/329-2500 🚇 Red Line: Grand 🚌 36

EMBASSY SUITES

embassysuiteschicago.com

The 367 suites are in a good location for Michigan Avenue shopping and River North nightlife. Substantial buffet breakfast and a free evening cocktail party included.

⊞ E8 ⊠ 600 N. State Street ☎ 312/943-3800 🚇 Red Line: Grand 🚌 36

THE GODFREY HOTEL

godfreyhotelchicago.com

This contemporary yet comfortable hotel, in a quiet area north of downtown, has a modern vibe, free WiFi and a killer view from its stylish rooftop bar.

⊞ D7 ⊠ 127 W. Huron Street ☎ 312/649-2000 🚇 Red, Brown and Purple Lines: Chicago 🚌 52, 56, 66

HAMPTON INN CHICAGO DOWNTOWN/MAGNIFICENT MILE

hamptoninn3.hilton.com

Any Hampton Inn in downtown Chicago is good value, since it includes free WiFi and a full complimentary breakfast. The Downtown/Magnificent Mile location has a seasonal rooftop pool plus business and fitness centers.

⊞ F7 ⊠ 160 E. Huron Street ☎ 312/706-0888 🚇 Red Line: Chicago 🚌 3, 10, 26, 125, 143, 146, 147, 148, 151

HOMEWOOD SUITES BY HILTON

homewoodsuiteschicago.com

These comfortable apartment rooms are some of the best value in town; breakfast included, free WiFi, business center access, a pool and fitness center, and complimentary snacks and drinks four nights a week. Many rooms have grand views of the Wrigley Building.

⊞ F7 ⊠ 40 East Grand Avenue ☎ 312/644-2222 🚇 Red Line: Chicago 🚌 29, 36

HOTEL ALLEGRO

allegrochicago.com

This well-established Loop hotel, known for its whimsical yet luxurious decor, has undergone a major renovation.

⊞ E9 ⊠ 171 W. Randolph Street ☎ 312/236-0123; 800/643-1500 🚇 Brown, Orange Lines: Randolph/Wells 🚌 37

HOTEL MONACO

monaco-chicago.com

Stylish striped wallpaper and offbeat colors provide zip to this 192-room boutique hotel in the Loop. Request a

room with a window seat to enjoy the view. Free WiFi and a complimentary wine reception nightly.

➕ F9 ✉ 225 N. Wabash Avenue
☎ 866/610-0081 🚇 Brown, Green, Orange Lines: State, Lake 🚌 29

HOTEL SAX CHICAGO

hotelsaxchicago.com

The lobby, bar and all 353 guest rooms of this former House of Blues Hotel were remodeled in 2007. While the rooms are stylish, most visitors stay here because it's adjacent to six restaurants, an upscale "bowling lounge," the Crunch gym and the House of Blues restaurant and club.

➕ E9 ✉ 333 N. Dearborn ☎ 312/245-0333; 877/569-3742 🚇 Red Line: Grand 🚌 22

KINZIE HOTEL

amalfihotelchicago.com

Near downtown and the Magnificent Mile, this Italian-style boutique hotel serves a complimentary breakfast and nightly hors d'oeuvres.

➕ E9 ✉ 20 W. Kinzie Street ☎ 312/395-9000; 877/262-5341 🚇 Red Line: Grand 🚌 22

MILLENNIUM KNICKER-BOCKER HOTEL

millenniumhotels.com

First built in 1927, its Martini Bar and Crystal Ballroom retain a feel for that era, although its 305 rooms are 21st-century standard.

➕ F6 ✉ 163 East Walton Place ☎ 312/751-8100 🚇 Red Line: Chicago 🚌 145, 146, 147, 151

RENAISSANCE CHICAGO

marriott.com

A great Loop location, 520 spacious rooms and 40 suites make this hotel a good choice. Facilities include an indoor pool and a fitness center.

➕ E9 ✉ 1 W. Wacker Drive ☎ 800/468-3571; 312/372-7200 🚇 Red Line: Lake, State; Brown, Green Lines: State 🚌 2, 10, 11, 44

SOFITEL CHICAGO WATER TOWER

sofitel.com

Striking glass hotel from French hoteliers Sofitel with good views of the John Hancock and a smart Mag Mile locale. Modern but comfortable furnishings in the rooms.

➕ F7 ✉ 20 E. Chestnut Street ☎ 312/324-4000 🚇 Red Line: Chicago 🚌 22, 66

TREMONT HOTEL

tremontchicago.com

This elegant, 130-room, Tudor-style hotel is close to Michigan Avenue.

➕ F7 ✉ 100 E. Chestnut Street ☎ 312/751-1900 🚇 Red Line: Chicago 🚌 145, 146, 147, 151

THE WHITEHALL

thewhitehallhotel.com

First opened in the 1920s, this 222-room hotel now has English-style furniture and modern amenities.

➕ F7 ✉ 105 E. Delaware Place ☎ 312/944-6300; 866/753-4081 🚇 Red Line: Chicago 🚌 145, 146, 147, 151

THE PLACE TO BE SEEN

Two W Hotels make seeing and being seen as much a part of the stay as a night's rest. The W Hotel Lakeshore (✉ 644 N. Lake Shore Drive ☎ 312/943-9200) harbors the intimate Whiskey Sky bar on an upper floor with skyline views for a change of scenery from the beautiful people. And the W Hotel City Center (✉ 172 W. Adams Street ☎ 312/332-1200) in the Loop draws the after-work crowd with a DJ (whotels.com).

Luxury Hotels

PRICES
Expect to pay between $250 and $650 or more for a luxury hotel.

ROOFTOP BARS
Chicago's swankiest hotels have gorgeous rooftop bars. Chicago Athletic Association Hotel, LondonHouse Hotel and theWit are among the busiest, the most scenic—and the priciest.

CHICAGO ATHLETIC ASSOCIATION HOTEL

chicagoathletichotel.com

Once a men's athletic club, this architecturally stunning downtown building was meticulously restored and made into a unique and gorgeous hotel with a game room, indoor pool and free bike rentals. The crown jewel is Cindy's, its rooftop restaurant and bar with killer views of Millennium Park.

🏁 F9 ✉ 12 S. Michigan Avenue ☎ 312/940-3552 🚇 Blue Line: Washington; Orange Line: Randolph/Wabash 🚌 146

THE DRAKE

thedrakehotel.com

The ornate Gold Coast Ballroom is evidence that The Drake was modeled on an Italian Renaissance palace. Some of the 535 rooms have lake views.

🏁 F6 ✉ 140 E. Walton Place ☎ 312/787-2200; 800/553-7253 🚇 Red Line: Chicago 🚌 145, 146, 147, 151

FAIRMONT HOTEL

fairmont.com/chicago

Winning views over Grant Park, the city and the lake; the 692 rooms are comfortable and tasteful. Use of health club.

🏁 F9 ✉ 200 N. Columbus Drive ☎ 312/565-8000; 866/540-4408 🚇 Brown, Orange Lines: State, Lake 🚌 4

THE LANGHAM CHICAGO

langhamhotels.com

Ranked as one of the best hotels in the US, The Langham sits along a scenic, riverfront spot in the city's center. Besides attentive service and spacious,

modern rooms, the indoor pool has shimmering lights on the ceiling, and the restaurant, Travelle Kitchen + Bar, is among the best in the city.

🏁 F9 ✉ 330 N. Wabash Avenue ☎ 312/923-9988 🚇 Brown, Green, Red, Pink, Purple Lines: Grand; Blue Line: Clark/Lake 🚌 121

PARK HYATT CHICAGO

parkchicago.hyatt.com

The best rooms, and the hotel's highly regarded NoMI restaurant, peer directly over the Historic Water Tower. Fine art complements the modern interiors.

🏁 F7 ✉ 800 N. Michigan Avenue ☎ 312/335-1234 🚇 Red Line: Chicago 🚌 66, 143, 144, 145, 146, 151

THE PENINSULA CHICAGO

chicago.peninsula.com

A gilded link in the Asia-based chain, the Peninsula Chicago has a lap pool with skyline views, a spa, luxurious rooms and exemplary service to match.

🏁 F7 ✉ 108 E. Superior Street ☎ 312/337-2888; 866/288-8889 🚇 Red Line: Chicago 🚌 143, 144, 145, 146, 151

RITZ-CARLTON CHICAGO

fourseasons.com/chicagorc

Whim-catering hotel popular with celebrities. The restaurant is a stand out and the locale is great for shoppers.

🏁 F7 ✉ 160 E. Pearson Street ☎ 312/266-1000; 800/621-6906 🚇 Red Line: Chicago 🚌 143, 144, 145, 146, 151

Use this section to familiarize yourself with travel to and within Chicago. Planning can help save money: The multiday visitor's pass allowing unlimited trips on the mass transit system is sold in advance.

Planning Ahead	114–115
Getting There	116–117
Getting Around	118–119
Essential Facts	120–123
Timeline	124–125

Planning Ahead

When To Go

June, July and August are the busiest months, but the weather can be tryingly hot. May, September and October are better months to visit, with fewer crowds and warm but less extreme weather. Events and festivals take place year-round. Major conventions in May, September, October and November cause hotel space to be scarce.

TIME

Chicago is one hour behind New York, two hours ahead of Los Angeles and six hours behind the UK.

AVERAGE DAILY MAXIMUM TEMPERATURES

JAN	FEB	MAR	APR	MAY	JUN	JUL	AUG	SEP	OCT	NOV	DEC
22°F	26°F	37°F	49°F	59°F	69°F	74°F	72°F	65°F	53°F	40°F	27°F
-6°C	-3°C	3°C	9°C	15°C	21°C	23°C	22°C	18°C	12°C	4°C	-3°C

Spring (mid-March to May) Very changeable; sometimes snow, sometimes sun, but generally mild.

Summer (June to mid-September) Varies from warm to very hot, sometimes uncomfortably so with high humidity.

Autumn (mid-September to October) Though changeable, it is often mild with sunny days.

Winter (November to mid-March) Often very cold with heavy snow and strong winds. Winds can be strong any time and particularly cold when, usually in winter, they come from the north.

WHAT'S ON

January/February *Chinese New Year:* In Chinatown.

March *St. Patrick's Day:* The city (including the Chicago River) turns green, and there's a parade through the Loop.

April *Baseball season opens. Chicago Antiques and Fine Art Fair.*

May *Polish Constitution Day* (first Sat): Chicago's Polish Americans celebrate with a parade and events focusing on Polish culture.
Wright Plus: See inside Oak Park homes designed by Frank Lloyd Wright.

June *Chicago Blues Festival*: Local and international artists perform in Grant Park. *Printer's Row Lit fest*: Used-book shops host events. *Chicago Gospel Festival*: Gospel music in Millennium Park.

July *Taste of Chicago*: Five-day feeding frenzy, thousands sample dishes from city restaurants.
Independence Day (Jul 4): Special events include fireworks at Navy Pier.

August *Ravinia Festival* (mid-June to Labor Day): Two months of the Chicago Symphony Orchestra, pop, folk and rock music, with picnicking on the lawns.
Chicago Air & Water Show: Spectacular stunts performed along the lakefront.

September *Chicago Jazz Festival*: Jazz stars headline free concerts in Grant Park.

October *Chicago Marathon.*

November/December *Festival of Lights:* Lights along the Magnificent Mile.

Chicago Online

cityofchicago.org
The city government website. Chicagoans use this to pay their bills and make complaints, but it holds plenty of interest to visitors.

choosechicago.com
Part of the above, but aimed more squarely at visitors.

enjoyillinois.org
Official site of the Illinois Office of Tourism.

chicagotribune.com
The online version of Chicago's biggest-circulation daily newspaper.

Chicago.Eater.com
An up-to-date, reliable website packed with restaurant reviews and news about Chicago's restaurants.

chicagoreader.com
The website of the city's long-established alter-native weekly newspaper, the *Chicago Reader*, with a different slant on city affairs and its own recommendations for entertainment.

chicago.metromix.com
Chicago edition of a national site providing informative listings, covering events, museums, dining, nightlife and more.

CTABusTracker.com
Helps you find out how far away your bus is—especially valuable when the weather's bad.

timeoutchicago.com
A glossy, edgy magazine with listings, trend pieces and feature stories on special events.

urchicago.com
This online magazine has features, interviews and expresses opinion about all things media, arts and performance in Chicago.

USEFUL SITES

fodors.com
A complete travel-planning site. Research prices and the weather; reserve air tickets, cars and rooms; ask questions (and get answers) from fellow visitors; and find links to other sites.

transitchicago.com
The website of the Chicago Transit Authority explains all there is to know about using the city's buses and El trains, the fares and ticket types, with route maps that can be downloaded and lots more.

Getting There

ENTRY REQUIREMENTS

Visitors to Chicago from outside the US require a machine-readable passport, valid for at least six months. Passports issued on or after October 26, 2004 must include a biometric identifier; UK passports already issued will still qualify for up to 90 days visa-free travel in the visa-waiver scheme. Visitors using the visa-waiver program must register their details online before traveling. Check the current situation before you leave (US Embassy visa information ☎ 202/643-4000; usembassy.gov; British Embassy in the US britainusa.com).
Be sure to leave plenty of time to clear security as the levels of checks are constantly being stepped up.

AIRPORTS

Chicago's O'Hare International Airport is 17 miles (27km) northwest of the Loop and takes all international flights and most domestic flights. Midway Airport, 8 miles (13km) southwest of the Loop, is primarily a domestic hub but also handles international travel.

FROM O'HARE INTERNATIONAL AIRPORT

For information on O'Hare International Airport, call 773/686-3700 or visit ohare.com. Continental Airport Express (tel 888/284-3826, airportexpress.com) runs minibuses between O'Hare and the Loop every 10–15 minutes 6am–11.30pm (fare $27; journey time 60 minutes). Pick them up from outside the arrivals terminal. Make a reservation for the trip from your hotel to the airport.

Chicago Transit Authority (tel 888/968-7282, transitchicago.com) operates Blue Line trains between O'Hare and the Loop (24 hours; journey time 45 minutes; fare $2.25). Follow the signs from the arrivals hall to the station. However, it is safer to take a taxi late at night from either airport. Taxis wait outside the arrivals terminal and the fare to the Loop or nearby hotels is about $35–$40.

ARRIVING AT MIDWAY AIRPORT

For information about Midway Airport, call 773/838-0600 or visit ohare.com. Continental Airport Express runs minibuses to the Loop every 15 minutes 6am–10.30pm (fare around

$20–$30; journey time 60 minutes). Pick the minibus up from outside Door 3 located on the lower level.

Chicago Transit Authority runs Orange Line trains to the Loop 5am–11.30pm (fare $2.25; journey time 30 minutes). Taxis wait at the arrivals terminal. The fare to the Loop or nearby hotels is approximately $45.

ARRIVING BY BUS
Greyhound buses (tel 800/231-2222; 312/408-5821, greyhound.com) arrive at 630 W. Harrison Street, six blocks southwest of the Loop. MegaBus (tel 877-462/6342, 773/890-6300, megabus.com), which serves eight Midwestern states with budget-priced fares, stops at Union Station on the east side of S. Canal Street, between Jackson Boulevard and Adams Street.

ARRIVING BY CAR
Chicago has good Interstate access: I-80 and I-90 are the major east–west routes; I-55 and I-57 arrive from the south. I-94 runs through the city linking the north and south suburbs. To reach the Loop from O'Hare airport use I-90/94. From Midway airport take I-55, linking with the northbound I-90/94 for the Loop. Journeys take from 45 to 90 minutes and 30 to 60 minutes respectively depending on traffic and weather. Try to avoid rush hours, 7–9am and 4–7pm.

There are more than half-dozen auto rental agencies at both O'Hare and Midway. Rates usually start in the range of $70 to $100 per day, $150 to $200 per week, with fuel as an extra charge. Check agencies for local specials.

ARRIVING BY TRAIN
Amtrak trains (tel 800/872-7245; 312/655-2385, amtrak.com) use Chicago's Union Station, junction of W. Adams and S. Canal streets. Amtrak can also be a great option for visitors traveling beyond Chicago. Trains serve the entire country.

CHICAGO GREETERS

The Chicago Office of Tourism's Department of Cultural Affairs runs a program to match volunteer residents with inquiring visitors. Chicago Greeters won't meet you at the airport, nor even on the day that you arrive, but by prior arrangement will spend two to four hours showing you around the city and providing an insider's point of view. The service is free but requires a seven-day advance registration via the website chicagogreeter. com. Greeters will escort one to six visitors on the itinerary of their choice ranging from outings themed to food or history or itineraries that look at a specific neighborhood.

Getting Around

DRIVING IN CHICAGO

Driving in the city is stressful: Use public transportation. Many hotels have parking lots, otherwise overnight parking is difficult and very costly. During the day, street parking is often limited to two hours; spaces in the Loop are near impossible to find.

VISITORS WITH DISABILITIES

Legislation aimed at improving access for visitors with disabilities in Chicago means that all recently built structures have to provide disabled access; the newer they are, the stricter the rules. Many older buildings, including most hotels, have been converted to ensure they comply. Both airports are accessible, as are many CTA buses and El stations. For details log on to transitchicago.com or cityofchicago.org/disabilities.

Much of Chicago can be explored on foot. To travel between neighborhoods use the network of buses and El (elevated) trains, which travel above and below ground. Many El trains operate 24-hours a day. Best value over many journeys are the Visitor Pass tickets valid for 1–7 days (cost $10–$28). Buy them from the airport, CTA stations, from major museums and the Visitor Information center (for information call 888/968-7282 or visit transitchicago.com/travel_information). Cash and multi-use plastic cards can be used. Taxis wait outside hotels, conference halls and major El stations, or can be hailed. Uber and Lyft ride services are easily available, using their companies' apps.

● If traveling outside the Loop at night, it is best to take a taxi rather than public transportation.
● Metra commuter trains are best for visiting some areas (metrarail.com).
● For information on the El and buses contact Chicago Transit Authority on 888/968-7282 or Metra on 312/322-6900; 312/322-6777.

THE EL

● Fare: $2.25 cash, $2 with card, plus 25¢ transfer. Transfer to a different line (or to a bus) within two hours: 25¢ (free within Loop). A second transfer within the same two hours is free. Children 7–11 ride for $1 cash, 85¢ with card, plus 15¢ transfer. Kids under age 6 travel free.
● Plastic transit cards are the simplest way to pay fares. Cash is an alternative. Cards are dispensed for cash, credit cards or debit cards from automated machines. Replenish existing cards as needed at the same machines.
● Visitor passes valid for 1 day ($10), 3 days ($20), 7 days ($28) or 30 days ($100) permit unlimited rides on buses and trains. The pass activates the first time you use it and is good for the consecutive number of calendar days shown on the front of the pass. You can order them before you arrive at the CTA website (transitchicago.com) or buy them at many hotels, Chicago visitor centers and O'Hare and Midway CTA stations.

- Many stations have only automatic ticket machines.
- Eight color-coded lines run through the city and converge on the Loop.
- On weekdays 6am–7pm, some trains stop only at alternate stations, plus all major stations. Station announcements will alert you to the change.
- Many trains run 24 hours; frequency is reduced on weekends and during the night. Several lines suspend service between roughly 1am and 5am.
- Some stations are closed weekends.

BUSES

- Fare: $2 with a transit card, $2.25 with cash. Transfer to a different route (or to the El) within two hours: 25¢. Second transfer as for the El.
- Plastic transit cards are the simplest way to pay fares (especially for the El). They are sold at some CTA train stations and Visitor Information centers.

SCHEDULE AND MAP INFORMATION

- CTA maps showing El and bus routes are available from El station fare booths.
- Bus routes are shown at stops.
- The CTA website (transitchicago.com) contains all schedules and maps and offers directions on how to get to popular tourist attractions.

TAXIS

- Fares are $3.25 for the first mile and $1.80 for each additional mile. The second additional passenger costs $1 and each further additional passenger costs 50¢. Midway- and O'Hare-bound trips cost an extra $1. Airport arrival/departure tax $2.
- Hotel, restaurant and nightclub staff will order a taxi on request or you can phone: Checker (tel 312/243-2537), Flash (tel 773/561-4444 or Yellow (tel 312/829-4222 or text 312/300-6894).

GOING BY WATER

In spring and summer the Chicago Water Taxi (☎ 312/337-1446; chicagowatertaxi.com) offers a ferry service from 6.30am to sundown. There are seven stops along the Chicago River: Madison Street, LaSalle Street, Michigan Avenue, Clark Street/Riverwalk, North Avenue/Sheffield, Chicago Avenue and Chinatown. One-way fares cost from $4 to $6 ($1 more at weekends); day pass $8 weekdays or $10.00 weekends.

MAPPING CHICAGO

Most of Chicago is laid out on a grid system with ground zero at State, which runs north–south, and Madison, east–west, in the Loop. Each block number changes by 100 with eight blocks equaling roughly one mile (1.6km). For instance, 800 N. State Street means the location is eight blocks north of the baseline intersection, while 110 E. Madison lies on the second block east of it. Even number addresses belong to the north or west side of a street; odd numbers mean the location is on the south or east side of a street.

Essential Facts

TRAVEL INSURANCE

Travel insurance is essential for the US because of the astronomical cost of any kind of medical treatment. Check your insurance policy and buy a supplementary policy if needed. A minimum of $1 million medical cover is recommended. Choose a policy that also includes trip cancellation, baggage loss and document loss.

MONEY

Dollar bills (notes) come in denominations of $1, $5, $10, $20, $50 and $100; coins are 25¢ (a quarter), 10¢ (a dime), 5¢ (a nickel) and 1¢ (a penny).

CUSTOMS REGULATIONS

● Duty-free allowances include 1 liter of alcoholic spirits or wine (no one under 21 may bring alcohol into the US), 200 cigarettes or 100 cigars, and up to $800-worth of gifts.
● Some medication bought over the counter abroad may be prescription-only in the US and may be confiscated. Bring a doctor's certificate for essential medication.
● It is forbidden to bring food, seeds and plants into the US.

ELECTRICITY

● The electricity supply is 110 volts; 60 cycles AC current.
● US appliances use two-prong plugs. European appliances require an adaptor.

ETIQUETTE

● Smoking is banned in all public buildings, restaurants, bars and on public transportation.
● Tipping is voluntary, but the following are usually expected: 15 percent-plus in restaurants; 15–20 percent for taxis; $1 per bag for a hotel porter.

INTERNATIONAL NEWSAGENTS

● Overseas newspapers and magazines can be found at Barnes & Noble.

MEDICAL TREATMENT

● For doctors, ask hotel staff or the Chicago Medical Society (tel 312/670-2550).
● In an emergency go to a hospital with a 24-hour emergency room, such as Northwestern Memorial Hospital at 251 E. Huron Street (tel 312/926-2000).
● If in need of dental care, the Chicago Dental Society (tel 312/836-7300) will refer you to a dentist in your area.

MEDICINES

● Pharmacies are listed in Yellow Pages. Visitors from Europe will find many familiar medicines under unfamiliar names. Some drugs available

over the counter at home, are prescription-only in the US.

● If you use medication bring a supply (but note the warning in Customs Regulations, ▷ 120). If you intend to buy prescription drugs in the US, bring a note from your doctor.
● There are many late-night and 24-hour pharmacies around the city, including Jewel-Osco (1224 S. Wabash, tel 312/663-0580), and two branches of Walgreens (757 N. Michigan Avenue, tel 312/664-8686; and at 641 N. Clark Street, tel 312/587-1416).

MONEY MATTERS

● Most banks have ATMs, which accept credit cards registered in other countries that are linked to the Cirrus or Plus networks. Ensure your personal identification number is valid in the US: four- and six-figure numbers are usual.
● Credit cards are widely accepted.
● US dollar traveler's checks function like cash in most shops; $20 and $50 denominations are most useful. Seeking to exchange these (or foreign currency) at a bank can be difficult and commissions can be high.
● A 10.25 percent sales tax is added to marked retail prices, except on groceries and prescription drugs.
● A Chicago CityPASS or a Go Chicago Card offer multiple discounts to major tourist destinations (go to smartdestinations.com or citypass.com/chicago).

NEWSPAPERS AND MAGAZINES

● Major daily newspapers are the *Chicago Tribune* and the tabloid *Chicago Sun-Times* (international, national and local stories).
● Best of several free weeklies is the *Chicago Reader*.
● Glossy monthly magazines such as the *Chicago* reflect the interests of well-heeled Chicagoans. The *Windy City Times* pitches to the LGBT community.
● Free magazines such as *Where Chicago,* and found in hotel lobbies, are aimed at tourists.

TOURIST OFFICES

The visitor information centers are in the lower level of the Macy's building, ✉ 111 N. State Street ☎ 312/781-4483, and at Millennium Park Welcome Center ✉ 201 E. Randolph Street, or Navy Pier Guest Services ✉ 600 E. Grand Avenue. Or visit ChooseChicago.com

NATIONAL HOLIDAYS

● New Year's Day (Jan 1)
● Martin Luther King Day (third Mon in Jan)
● President's Day (third Mon in Feb)
● Memorial Day (last Mon in May)
● Independence Day (Jul 4)
● Labor Day (first Mon in Sep)
● Columbus Day (second Mon in Oct)
● Veteran's Day (Nov 11)
● Thanksgiving Day (fourth Thu in Nov)
● Christmas Day (Dec 25)

EMERGENCY PHONE NUMBERS

● Fire, police or ambulance ☎ 911 (no money required)
● Rape Crisis Hotline ☎ 888/293-2080

LOST AND FOUND

● O'Hare International Airport ☎ 773/686-2385
● Items lost in a cab: Department of Consumer Services ☎ 312/746-7100
● The El and buses: Chicago Transit Authority ☎ 888/968-7282; Metra ☎ 312/322-7819
⏰ Daily 7.45am–1am

OPENING HOURS

● Stores: Mon–Sat from 9 or 10 until 6 or 7. Most stores are also open Sun noon–6. Department stores and malls keep longer hours; bookshops may open in the evenings.
● Banks: Mon–Fri from 9–3, with some branches open later once a week.

POST OFFICES

● Minimum charge for sending a postcard anywhere outside the US is $1.15.
● To find the nearest post office, look in the phone book or ask at your hotel. Most open Mon–Fri 8.30–5, Sat 8.30–1.

SENSIBLE PRECAUTIONS

● By day, the Loop and major areas of interest to visitors are relatively safe. Some tourist sights involve journeys through unwelcoming areas; be especially wary if traveling through the South Side and West Side. Discuss your itinerary with hotel staff and heed their advice.
● After dark, stay in established nightlife areas. River North and River West, Rush and Division streets, and Lakeview/Wrigleyville are fairly safe if you use common-sense precautions. If you're alone, wait for a cab inside a club or restaurant, or where staff can see you.
● Neighborhoods can change character within a few blocks. Stick to safe, busy streets.
● Carry shoulder bags strapped across your chest. Keep belongings within sight and reach.
● Store valuables in your hotel's safe and never carry more money than you need.
● Replacing a stolen passport begins with a visit or phone call to your nearest consular office.
● Report any stolen item to the nearest police precinct (see the phone book). It is unlikely that stolen goods will be recovered, but the police will fill in the forms your insurance company needs.

STUDENT VISITORS

● An International Student Identity Card (ISIC) reduces admission prices to many attractions.

● Anyone aged under 21 is forbidden to buy or drink alcohol and may be denied admission to some nightclubs.

TELEPHONES
● Pay telephones may still be found in public places but are quite rare. Rates vary depending on the provider but calls may be expensive.
● Calls from hotel rooms are usually more expensive than those from public phones.
● Many businesses have toll-free numbers, prefixed with 800, 866 or 888.
● Most US phones use touch-tone dialing, enabling callers to access extensions directly.
● To call Chicago from the UK dial 001 followed by the full number. To call the UK from Chicago dial 011-44 and omit the first zero from the area code.

TOILETS
● Most department stores, malls and hotel lobbies have adequate toilets.

TV AND RADIO
Chicago's main TV channels are 2 WBBM (CBS); 5 WMAQ (NBC); 7 WLS (ABC); 9 WGN (local WB affiliate); 11 WTTW (PBS); 32 WFLD (Fox).
Radio stations include:
● Classical: WFMT 98.7FM
● Country: WUSN 99.5FM
● National Public Radio: WBEZ 91.5FM
● News: WBBM 780AM
● R&B: WCI 107.5FM
● Talk radio and local sports: WGN 720AM; WSCR 670AM; WLS 890AM; ESPN CHICAGO AM1000

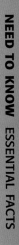
TRAVELING WITH CHILDREN

Chicago is a destination that welcomes children. Classic sights like the Willis Tower Observatory, Navy Pier, Shedd Aquarium, Field Museum, Museum of Science and Industry and the Chicago Children's Museum delight all ages, but especially kids. Furthermore, adults don't have to sacrifice their own interests to those of a child. The Art Institute of Chicago runs an excellent visitor's program for children; check their website (artic.edu) for a month-by-month guide to the activities. The Crown Fountain in Millennium Park is a popular spot for kids to play in summer in the water while families tour the grounds. When rest is required for little legs, go passive sightseeing by riding the El or taking a water taxi.

CONSULATES

Germany	✉ 676 N. Michigan Avenue, Suite 3200	☎ 312/202-0480
Ireland	✉ 1 E. Wacker Drive, Suite 1820	☎ 312/337-2700
UK	✉ 625 N. Michigan Avenue, Suite 2200	☎ 312/970-3800
Portugal	✉ D10, 10 S. Wacker Drive, 28th Floor	☎ 312/345-1149
Spain	✉ F9, 180 N Michigan Avenue # 1500	☎ 312/782-4588

Timeline

NEED TO KNOW TIMELINE

WINDY CITY

In 1893 Chicago hosted the World's Columbian Exposition. The hyperbole of business leaders caused one journalist to describe Chicago as "the windy city," an enduring epithet.

THE HAYMARKET RIOT

Heavy-handed police tactics in a series of labor disputes prompted a group of German-born anarchists to organize a protest rally on May 4, 1886, in Haymarket Square. A bomb thrown from the crowd exploded among the police lines; the explosion and the police use of firearms killed seven people and wounded 150. Seven anarchists received death sentences. In 1893, a full pardon was granted to three imprisoned anarchists, due to the lack of evidence linking any of the anarchists to the bomb.

1673 Missionary Jacques Marquette and explorer Louis Joliet discover the 1.5 mile (2.4km) Native-American portage trail linking the Mississippi River and the Great Lakes—the site of future Chicago.

1779–81 Trapper and trader Jean Baptiste Point du Sable, a Haitian, becomes the first non-native settler.

1812 Fort Dearborn, one of several forts protecting trade routes, is attacked by Native Americans.

1830 Chicago is selected as the site of a canal linking the Great Lakes and the Mississippi.

1870 Chicago's population reaches 330,000 from 30,000 in 1850. Many arrivals are Irish, who find work building the railways.

1871 The Great Fire kills 300 people.

1894 A strike at the Pullman rail company unites black and white workers for the first time.

1906 Upton Sinclair's novel *The Jungle* focuses national attention on the conditions endured by workers in the notorious Union Stockyards.

1908 Chicago Cubs win baseball's World Series for a second successive year.

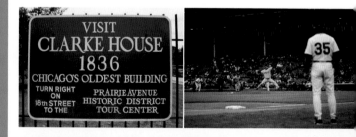

VISIT
CLARKE HOUSE
1836
CHICAGO'S OLDEST BUILDING
TURN RIGHT ON 18th STREET TO THE
PRAIRIE AVENUE HISTORIC DISTRICT TOUR CENTER

1914 With World War I, Chicago's black population increases, as African-Americans from the Deep South move north to industrial jobs.

1919–33 Prohibition. Chicago's transport links make it a natural place for alcohol manufacture and distribution. Armed crime mobs thrive.

1950s In South Side clubs, rhythmic and electrified Chicago blues evolves.

1955 Richard J. Daley is elected mayor and dominates Chicago political life for 21 years.

1968 Police attack anti-Vietnam War protesters in Grant Park during the Democratic National Convention.

1974 Completion of Sears Tower (now Willis Tower), the world's tallest building until 1996.

1992 A collapsing wall causes the Chicago River to flood the Loop.

2009 Illinois senator and Chicago resident Barack Obama is sworn in as the 44th President of the United States.

2011 Richard M. Daley, City's longest serving Mayor (22 years), leaves office and Rahm Emanuel becomes the 55th Mayor of Chicago.

2016 The Chicago Cubs baseball team wins the World Series for the first time in 108 years.

GANGSTERS

Intended to encourage sobriety and family life, Prohibition (1919–33) provided a great stimulus to organized crime. The exploits of Chicago-based gangsters such as Al Capone became legendary. Though depicted frequently on films and TV, shoot-outs between rival gangs were rare. An exception was the 1929 Valentine's Day Massacre, when Capone's gang eliminated their archrivals in a hail of machine-gun fire. Wealthy enough to bribe corruptible politicians and police, the gangsters seemed invincible, but the gangster era—though not necessarily the gangs—ended with Capone's imprisonment in 1931 and the repeal of Prohibition.

From left to right: directions to Clarke House; a baseball game in progress at Wrigley Field; an old copy of the Chicago Daily Tribune; *the Hyatt Center soars skyward*

Index

A

accommodation 107–112
 bed-and-breakfast 109
 hotels 108–112
Adler Planetarium and
 Astronomy Museum 8,
 42–43
airports 116–117
American Writers Museum 30
architecture 5, 16, 24, 50,
 100, 102
art and antiques 10, 12, 34,
 60–61, 75, 103
Art Institute of Chicago 8,
 44–45
ATMs 121

B

banks 121, 122
baseball 11, 101
bed-and-breakfast 109
bike tours 84
biking 8, 84
blues 35, 53, 76, 77, 86
book fair 33
book and music shops 11, 12,
 33, 34, 74, 103
Boystown 69, 102
Buckingham Fountain 51
Bucktown 99
budget travellers 16, 109
Burnham, Daniel 4, 5, 27, 50,
 51, 64, 70
buses 119
 long-distance 117

C

360 Chicago 58
Carbide & Carbon Building
 24
Chess Pavilion 66
Chicago Architecture
 Foundation River Cruise
 8, 24
Chicago Board of Trade 32
Chicago Children's Musuem
 69
Chicago Cultural Center 30
Chicago Greeters 117
Chicago History Museum 69
Chicago River 24
Chicago Riverwalk 30
children's entertainment 16,
 123
Chinatown 90
Chinese New Year 93
Clarke House 87
classical music venues 35, 36
climate and seasons 114

clubs and bars
 see entertainment and
 nightlife
comedy shows 35, 67, 77
consulates 123
conventions 108
crafts 33
credit cards 121
customs regulations 120

D

dance, modern 53
department stores and malls 12
disabilities, visitors with 118
driving 117, 118
DuSable Museum of African
 American History 8, 85

E

eating out
 see where to eat
electricity 120
El train 8, 26, 118–119
emergency phone numbers
 121
entertainment and nightlife
 13, 16–18
 Farther Afield 104
 listings 115
 the Loop 35–36
 Museum Campus 53
 North Side 76–77
 South Side 93
Ernest Hemingway Museum
 102
events and festivals 53, 54,
 86, 93, 104, 114

F

Farther Afield 95–106
 entertainment and nightlife
 104
 map 96–97
 shopping 99, 103
 sights 98–102
 where to eat 106
fashion shopping 10, 12, 17,
 33, 34, 74, 75
Field Museum of Natural
 History 8, 46–47
food and drink
 food festival 54
 hot dogs 14, 79
 Indian 106
 liquor laws 77
 pizza 14, 80
 vegetarian food 38
 see also
 where to eat

football 51
Fourth Presbyterian Church
 69
Frank Lloyd Wright Home
 and Studio 8, 100
Frank Lloyd Wright Tour 102

G

gangsters 125
Garfield Park Conservatory
 102
Gehry, Frank 50
Glessner House 87
Gold Coast 70
Graceland Cemetery and
 Arboretum 102
Grant Park 51
Great Fire of 1871 4, 27

H

Hemingway, Ernest 102
Historic Water Tower 70, 73
history 124–125
Holy Name Cathedral 70
hotels 18, 108–112

I

insurance 120
International Museum of
 Surgical Sciences 70
itinerary 6–7

J

Jackson Park 90
James R. Thompson Center
 30
Jane Addams Hull-House
 Museum 90
jazz and blues 4, 11, 13, 35,
 53, 76, 86, 93, 104
John G. Shedd Aquarium 8,
 48–49
John Hancock Center 8, 13,
 58–59

L

lakefront, biking on the 8, 84
Lake Michigan 66
Lincoln Park Conservatory 71
Lincoln Park Zoo 8, 62–63
liquor laws 77
the Loop 20–38
 entertainment and nightlife
 35–36
 map 22–23
 shopping 33–34
 sights 24–31
 walk 32
 where to eat 37–38

Loop Public Sculpture 8, 25
lost and found 122

M
Magnificent Mile 8, 10, 13, 68, 73, 75
maps
    Farther Afield 96–97
    the Loop 22–23
    Museum Campus 40–41
    North Side 56–57
    South Side 82–83
Marina City Towers 24
Marquette Building 30
medical and dental treatment 120
medicines 120–121
Mies van der Rohe, Ludwig 5, 91
Millennium Park 8, 50
money 120, 121
Monroe Harbor 51
Museum Campus 39–54
    entertainment and nightlife 53
    map 40–41
    sights 42–51
    walk 52
    where to eat 54
Museum of Contemporary Art 71
Museum of Science and Industry 8, 88–89

N
national holidays 121
National Museum of Mexican Art 90
Navy Pier 8, 64–65
newspapers and magazines 120, 121
newspapers, online 115
North Avenue Beach 8, 66
North Side 55–80
    entertainment and nightlife 76–77
    map 56–57
    shopping 68, 74–75
    sights 58–72
    walk 73
    where to eat 78–80

O
Oak Street Beach 71
Old Town 71–72
opening hours 122
opera 35
Osaka Japanese Garden 92

P
parking 118
passports and visas 116, 122
Peggy Notebaert Nature Museum 72
performance poets 104
pharmacies 120–121
Picasso, Pablo 25
post offices 122
Prairie Avenue District 8, 87
Printer's Row 31, 33
public transportation 118–119

R
radio and TV 123
river buses 119
river cruises 24, 64
River North 8, 60–61
Robie House 91
Rookery 8, 27

S
safety, personal 122–123
sales tax 121
sculpture 25, 32, 50, 71
Second City 8, 67, 77
shopping 10–12, 17
    Farther Afield 99, 103
    the Loop 33–34
    North Side 68, 74–75
    opening hours 122
Smart Museum of Art 91
smoking etiquette 120
Soldier Field 51
South Side 81–94
    entertainment and nightlife 93
    map 82–83
    sights 84–91
    walk 92
    where to eat 94
souvenirs 11, 17
Spertus Institute and Museum 31
sporting memorabilia 11
street grid system 119
student visitors 122–123
Sullivan Center 31

T
taxis 119
telephones 123
The 606 102
theater 16, 35, 36, 65, 76, 77, 93, 104
ticket outlets 36
time differences 114
tipping 120

toilets 123
tourist information 115
tourist offices 121
train services 117
    see also El Train
travel arrangements 116–117
traveler's checks 121
travel passes 118
Tribune Tower 24, 72

U
University of Chicago 91

V
vegetarian food 38
views over the city 13, 32, 58–59
volleyball 66

W
walks
    the Loop 32
    Magnificent Mile 73
    Museum Campus 52
    South Side 92
water taxi 119
websites 115
where to eat 5, 14–15, 17, 18
    Farther Afield 106
    the Loop 37–38
    Museum Campus 54
    North Side 78–80
    South Side 94
Wicker Park/Bucktown 8, 99
Willis Tower 8, 13, 28–29, 32
"windy city" epithet 124
Wright, Frank Lloyd 5, 27, 100, 102
Wrigley Building 13, 24, 72
Wrigley Field 8, 11, 101

Z
zoo 8, 62–63

Titles in the Series

- Amsterdam
- Bangkok
- Barcelona
- Boston
- Brussels and Bruges
- Budapest
- Chicago
- Dubai
- Dublin
- Edinburgh
- Florence
- Hong Kong
- Istanbul
- Krakow
- Las Vegas
- Lisbon
- London
- Madrid
- Melbourne
- Milan
- Montréal
- Munich
- New York City
- Orlando
- Paris
- Rome
- San Francisco
- Seattle
- Shanghai
- Singapore
- Sydney
- Tokyo
- Toronto
- Venice
- Vienna
- Washington, D.C.